Growing In Christ

Sermons For
The Spring Season

Michael D. Wuchter
submitted by Shirley Dyer Wuchter

CSS Publishing Company, Inc., Lima, Ohio

Copyright © 2008 by
CSS Publishing Company, Inc.
Lima, Ohio

Most scripture quotations are from the New Revised Standard Version of the Bible, copy-right 1989 by the Division of Christian Education of the National Council of the Churches of Christ in the USA. Used by permission.

Scripture quotations marked (RSV) are taken from the Revised Standard Version of the Bible, copyrighted 1946, 1952 ©, 1971, 1973, by the Division of Christian Education of the National Council of the Churches of Christ in the USA. Used by permission.

Library of Congress Cataloging-in-Publication Data

Wuchter, Michael D.
    Growing in Christ : sermons for the spring season / Michael D. Wuchter.
        p. cm.
    ISBN 0-7880-2523-6 (perfect bound : alk. paper)
    1. Lenten sermons. 2. Easter—sermons. 3. Lutheran Church—Sermons. 4. Church year sermons. 5. Sermons, American—20th century. I. Title.

    BV4277.W83 2008
    252'.041—dc22

                                                                        2007040087

For more information about CSS Publishing Company resources, visit our website at www.csspub.com or email us at csr@csspub.com or call (800) 241-4056.

Cover design by Barbara Spencer
ISBN-13: 978-0-7880-2523-5
ISBN-10: 0-7880-2523-6

                                                        PRINTED IN USA

Dedicated to
Hannah Ruth Brown
born August 21, 2007,
the most recent member
of our growing family

Michael Wuchter's writing is a delight. His shifting and many-fac-
-eted themes return again and again to the essentials of Christian
faith for the individual, the community and society. Wuchter
preached with such detail and precision — how he must have held
the attention of those who came to listen. He looks with honesty
and candor at the fears, vanities, and injustice of our day and speaks
to them with the springtime promise of God's love.

> Ann E. Hafften
> Writer and editor
> Weatherford, Texas
> Author of *Waters from the Rock —*
> *Lutheran Voices from Palestine*

Michael's sermons are sheer poetry. They bring such a strong emo-
tional response for me that it is often days later that I realize the
theological and intellectual authenticity and integrity of these ser-
mons that had swept me off my feet emotionally. This is preaching
at its finest. They are like Michael was in his life: artistic, deeply
thoughtful, literate, engaging ... stories well told. And like the sea-
son these sermons were given in, spring, Michael's words often
surprise and delight, like the first daffodils and jonquils that are
not afraid to peek their heads out from under a late spring snow-
storm. As warden of the Cathedral College, home to the College of
Preachers, I know excellence in preaching when I encounter it.
Michael's sermons sing and dance.

> Howard R. Anderson
> President and Warden
> Cathedral College of Washington National
>   Cathedral
> Washington, DC

Michael Wuchter was a master of the English language and an excellent, excellent preacher.

Jerry L. Schmalenberger
Former President
Pacific Lutheran Theological Seminary

During Lent and Easter, the church moves from confession to forgiveness, from the entanglements of this world to freedom in Christ, from darkness to light. Michael Wuchter makes that same move in these twelve sermons. From the narratives of Genesis to a detailed explanation of the resurrection, from parades in France and Guatemala to hiking the Superior Trail, Wuchter takes us on the journey of God's grace. And as he says, this foray into God's love and mercy is "a grand adventure."

John D. Morris
Pastor, Prince of Peace Lutheran Church
Dublin, Ohio

These sermons carry us not only through the spring season but from the encounter of Adam and Eve with the snake to the time of our reflections anticipating death. In all of these arresting homilies, the personal, familial, societal, local/global connections to the gospel are powerfully expressed.

Daniel F. Martensen
Ecumenical Research Fellow,
Washington (DC) Theological Consortium
Former Director,
Dept. of Ecumenical Affairs, ELCA

Michael Wuchter's twin callings in parish and campus ministries come alive in these sermons. His concern for making the gospel relevant in a rapidly changing society are evident as one reads these messages based on sound biblical scholarship. This is great reading for all the people of God.

Edwin Ehlers
Retired Bishop
New Jersey Synod,
Evangelical Lutheran Church in America

Even though I've only had a couple days to look over the sermons for this book, I have found that it contains some of the best material I have ever read on communion, confirmation, and the holiness and power of our calling to befriend each other and all people we meet along the journey. Thanks for the reminders about who we are.

Carol Hertler
ELCA Pastor
Chillicothe, Ohio

Acknowledgments

This book is the third in a series of sermons organized by the church year. I am grateful to the members of my husband's parish after his death who were the first to request his sermons in print. Dave Benson, an author, editor, and friend of my husband's, stepped forward to lend his support to uphold the integrity of the sermons and to offer his expertise and encouragement to me.

Additionally, colleagues of my husband's at Wittenberg University in Springfield, Ohio, were instrumental in helping me persevere in my personal grief journey and simultaneously gave direction in pulling the books together for publication. My Lake Superior Writer's Association Memoir Group — Martha Aas, Kay Coventry, Jeanice Fontaine, Destri Irwin, Margaret Kinetz, Dorothy Lutz, and Dorothy Schilling — offered moral support and editorial tips. My Wednesday Morning Prayer Group at First Lutheran Church supported me in prayer.

Thanks to all the members of my family who quietly strengthened me as did my many friends. Gratitude goes to those who were given little time, yet submitted endorsements to my hard-working and amiable editor, Becky Allen, whose family was also growing during this time.

Ultimately, thanks be to God.

Table Of Contents

Introduction

My life story now revolves around the date of August 5, 2000. On that day, my life spun out of control and was so totally changed. My husband of almost 31 years, suddenly collapsed in my arms and took his final breath. We were in Namibia, Africa, about to meet a delegation of Lutherans with which we had been partnered in a church-to-church relationship. They were dedicating their new building the next day.

You can imagine how stunned that congregation was, as was his parish, First Lutheran Church, in Duluth, Minnesota. The shock waves extended to family and friends, to people in his former parish of Resurrection Lutheran Church in Hamilton Square, New Jersey, and to the students he shepherded during his eighteen years as Campus Pastor at Wittenberg University in Springfield, Ohio, and to acquaintances around the globe.

Since then, I have been on a journey of healing and I, like the title, have been growing with Christ. All my life, I have been associated with a church and have been an active member. There have been times when I have struggled in my faith, when I have wrestled with God, and when I have sought direction. But when Michael died, I was devastated. I did not doubt, however, that God was with me.

In building my life, after losing my most beloved friend, I found that my faith grew in depth and breadth. I gained a new sensitivity. I gained new insights. I grew in many ways that were complex and hard to define. But, like the season of Lent, when we often face more intentionally the hardships of Christ's life and death, we can emerge with a stronger, richer faith.

Michael's sermons in this collection that progress through Lent toward Easter and end with Holy Trinity Sunday deal with the key messages of our faith and help define important components, like communion and resurrection. As a pastor in a young church, as a college chaplain, and as a parish pastor, Michael was aware that people struggle to understand their faith and apply it to their daily lives. Here is a collection of sermons that can serve as an anchor, as a benchmark, as food for thought, as devotions, and as a tool or support in your growth in faith.

Interestingly, as this book was in its final phase, I was traveling to Montana in anticipation of my second grandchild being born. I knew I should be trusting God more as I thought of all the things that could go wrong. The best possible scenario evolved: my daughter and her husband, who live one-and-one-half miles from the nearest hospital, drove to Billings when contractions started on August 20. The hospital didn't admit them that night since she wasn't far enough along. The next day, however, after a good night's sleep, a healthy Hannah Ruth was born. My growing faith reminds me that God provides. It is with a grateful heart that I dedicate this book to my growing family.

— Shirley Dyer Wuchter
September 14, 2007
Duluth, Minnesota

Snake Talk

... then the Lord God formed man from the dust of the
ground, and breathed into his nostrils the breath of life;
and the man became a living being. And the Lord God
planted a garden in Eden, in the east; and there he put
the man whom he had formed. Out of the ground the
Lord God made to grow every tree that is pleasant to
the sight and good for food, the tree of life also in the
midst of the garden, and the tree of the knowledge of
good and evil.

A river flows out of Eden to water the garden, and
from there it divides and becomes four branches. The
name of the first is Pishon; it is the one that flows around
the whole land of Havilah, where there is gold; and the
gold of that land is good; bdellium and onyx stone are
there. The name of the second river is Gihon; it is the
one that flows around the whole land of Cush. The name
of the third river is Tigris, which flows east of Assyria.
And the fourth river is the Euphrates.

The Lord God took the man and put him in the
garden of Eden to till it and keep it. And the Lord God
commanded the man, "You may freely eat of every tree
of the garden; but of the tree of the knowledge of good
and evil you shall not eat, for in the day that you eat of
it you shall die."

Then the Lord God said, "It is not good that the
man should be alone; I will make him a helper as his
partner." So out of the ground the Lord God formed
every animal of the field and every bird of the air, and
brought them to the man to see what he would call them;
and whatever the man called every living creature, that
was its name. The man gave names to all cattle, and to

*the birds of the air, and to every animal of the field; but
for the man there was not found a helper as his partner.
So the Lord God caused a deep sleep to fall upon the
man, and he slept; then he took one of his ribs and closed
up its place with flesh. And the rib that the Lord God
had taken from the man he made into a woman and
brought her to the man. Then the man said,*

> *"This at last is bone of my bones
> and flesh of my flesh;
> this one shall be called Woman,
> for out of Man this one was taken."*

*Therefore a man leaves his father and his mother and
clings to his wife, and they become one flesh. And the
man and his wife were both naked, and were not
ashamed.*

*Now the serpent was more crafty than any other
wild animal that the Lord God had made. He said to
the woman, "Did God say, 'You shall not eat from any
tree in the garden'?" The woman said to the serpent,
"We may eat of the fruit of the trees in the garden; but
God said, 'You shall not eat of the fruit of the tree that
is in the middle of the garden, nor shall you touch it, or
you shall die.'" But the serpent said to the woman, "You
will not die; for God knows that when you eat of it your
eyes will be opened, and you will be like God, knowing
good and evil." So when the woman saw that the tree
was good for food, and that it was a delight to the eyes,
and that the tree was to be desired to make one wise,
she took of its fruit and ate; and she also gave some to
her husband, who was with her, and he ate. Then the
eyes of both were opened, and they knew that they were
naked; and they sewed fig leaves together and made
loin-cloths for themselves.* — Genesis 2:7—3:7

The season is Lent. It is a time to look deeply and honestly
within ourselves. Our first Bible lesson did just that this morning.
It was part of the Adam and Eve story from Genesis. This story
was not meant as ancient history. It is rather personal history, a
kind of biography of every person.

16

Adam and Eve. Their names are clues. Adam is Hebrew for "mankind — humanity." Eve means "life." The couple represents human life.

In the opening chapters of Genesis, various narratives are woven and welded together. The highly developed Eastern art of storytelling, using dramatic action and dialogue, is at its peak. The fragmented narrative that formed most of our Old Testament reading this morning used a number of symbolic concepts of Babylonian and Canaanite origin — "the rivers of paradise," "the shrewd serpent of evil," "the search for immortality through divine food," and "the tree of life." You can still find the "tree of life" pattern woven into Persian rugs and other oriental carpets.

The keys to today's story are the questions that are being asked: Why is total peace and harmony closed to human beings? What is evil? What is God's will?

The story we have is one that gives answers. God does not will evil. Mankind is mortal. Humanity has the freedom of decision that makes us human but is misused. Paradise is closed, folks.

Mankind is selfish, which goes against God's will, but God still cares.

These are key insights — ultimate truths — but nobody really listens to all that stuff or tries to understand it, or identify with it "until the snake talks." It is storytelling at its best. A fast-talking snake. The reptile is like E. F. Hutton. When the snake talks, people listen. Let's listen to this snake — he is talking to us.

The serpent is a subtle creature; he doesn't start out his spell by saying, "I am an atheistic psycho-monster, and I am going to take away your paradise, your innocence, your loyalty and faith to God, and turn everything all upside down."

No, he didn't (and doesn't) come on like that, because it would be easy to run away from a serpent like that. It would be like the devil in the movie *The Exorcist* — as subtle as a sledgehammer.

You could spot it a mile away. No, the real serpent is a subtle creature. He says instead, "Child, today we're going to discuss the ultimate things in a friendly manner. Relax.

"Did God, this God whom we all revere (even I, the serpent, honor him dearly) did our revered God really say there was some

17

tree in this huge garden that you were not to mess with? Oh, come on! My dear, I certainly do not want you to start doubting the judgment of God or God himself. Oh no! Just stop and reflect for a moment, not by way of opposition to God, but in the name of God, whether he could have said anything like that at all.

"After all, it would certainly be undivine of him to forbid you to eat of these trees! Do you think that God is so narrow-minded that he would not let you get near these unusually wonderful products of his creation in the midst of the garden? Is he the kind of God who does nothing but set up barriers, put on bridles, and post stop signs?

"Does it take me, the serpent, to explain to you that God is a God of the unlimited abundance of life? Why should anything that he himself made be bad and forbidden?"

The smooth-talking serpent goes on: "Did God forbid you to live your life to the full? Go grab for all the gusto you can. Did God forbid you to use all your instincts? Do you really think God would be so prim and legalistic? After all, he created you and your vitality the way it is. So everything you do is covered by the Creator!"

The serpent adds some embellishments. "Perhaps you are a person who has machines, bank accounts, and influence at your disposal. It tickles you to make a regular cult of your social prestige, to have people bowing and scraping before you and to make big splurges. Don't worry, as a serpent I have a few soothing words to say to you. Did God forbid you to think about yourself once in a while instead of your neighbor? Do you think he really demands that you limit your God and possibly even lose a little of your hard-earned dollars and position?

"Nonsense, my dear friend, my lovely lady, don't burden your conscience with such moral clichés! After all, who gave you what you have? Wasn't it providence that blessed you with business opportunities and economic miracles? Didn't you work darn hard for it? It was your brain. Why help those with less gray matter?"

The serpent can even quote from the Bible. "You shall not muzzle an ox while it is treading out the grain" (Deuteronomy 25:4). So in the name of the Bible, keep turning out the grain. "The ox comes first," says God, "and you are the ox, my dear Eve."

The serpent does not let up, "God is not at all a narrow-minded, moralistic God who is always getting in your way. Rather, he is the God of life, the God of abundance. Take everything you can get, for God is handing it out to you. Act according to the laws of life, even when they are cruel, for God made life. Take advantage of the rights of the stronger, for God is always on the side that has the heaviest artillery. Keep shoving down and climbing up; that's the way to get ahead. After all, that's what this life (God created) looks like! If anybody does the trampling, it's me, and if anybody gets trampled, it's going to be you. *C'est la vie* — and that's probably what he who made life is like, too."

The snake takes a breath and continues. "God put at our disposal the whole breadth of his creation: the multitude of plants and animals are at our service, the laws of nature are there to be explored and technologically utilized, and the whole cosmos is offered as our dominion. Only one spot in all this infinite expanse must remain taboo, inviolable, unreachable, and reserved to God himself, namely this one lovely tree. Come on, Eve, let's eat the fruit.

"This one paltry point cannot matter that much! What is this one apple compared with the peaches and melons and strawberries and avocadoes to which God has no objections? If you conform to God in 99 points out of 100 and more in the area he has assigned to you, surely, Eve, this one point in a thousand isn't going to upset your space with God!"

The serpent is playing fast and loose here. "The fact is that all of us have sectors in the territory of our lives that we are quite content to leave to God, but each of us also has an area that we will by no means let God approach. This point may be an ambition whereby I am determined to beat my way to success in my career at any price. It may be a feeling of superiority over another person, sex, or race. It may be a bottomless hatred toward one of my fellow humans that I literally nurse that gives me a kind of sensual pleasure and comes between God and me and robs me of my peace.

"God can have everything, but not this one thing! God can have my unselfish devotion and service. After all, I am an idealist! I will devote myself to a task totally and without regard for loss. I

19

am industrious and active. He can have it all — except this one thing.

"God can even have my neighborly love. I am good-hearted, I like people who like me, and I wouldn't hurt a fly. He can have my love for my neighbors; that isn't hard for me. He can have everything — except this one thing."

It's at this point that the serpent abandons his reserve and subtly lays his cards on the table.

Up to this time Eve had taken God seriously. She knew that when we are dealing with God, we are dealing with life and death; that our purpose and destiny in time and eternity is at stake.

The serpent says to her, "Surely it is sheer nonsense to think that God would let you die just because you don't take him so terribly in earnest, but rather just partly seriously. You will not die! The question of God is not that serious, my dear lady! All honor to your respect for him. I take my hat off to your display of piety, but really now, he's not that serious about it!

"Child, you take things too hard. God isn't that serious. I have no intention whatsoever of abolishing belief in God. By no means do I want to go that far. After all, we need something like religion, for example. You can say to your children, 'God is watching you'; and so in God you get a free babysitter, a free stick. Besides, there are moments, perhaps when you look up at the starry sky at the end of a beautiful vacation day, or in church on Christmas Eve, or Easter morning, or when a wedding procession moves up the aisle amid the sound of organ music — moments when you feel real religious, and I wouldn't want you to miss the emotional value of that.

"But naturally, you know that you cannot live by these emotional values alone. At most they are a kind of dessert, an after-dinner drink, a slight tonic effect. The main dish, the bread on which you really live, is your monthly income, your weekly wages, your school grades, or your professional status and personal power. If that were taken away from you, there would be the devil to pay. This would really be an awful threat; this would *really* be a matter of life and death.

"But what if religion were taken away — it certainly wouldn't be nice; but after all, a person can live without dessert if one has to." Well, that's enough snake talk.

Actually in the end, the snake is not too subtle, and this is the real serpent speaking. He is not exactly always speaking to us, because often we are the serpent. The serpent is a mythical expression of the self-destructive character of our own self-imposed separation from God. We are often the apple-swiping snake!

In our freedom, we are irresponsible. We isolate ourselves. We forget that God is not Grandfather Zeus. God is rather the power of *being*, the *creating center of purpose*; and everything we experience with God is closely interwoven with our relationship in love to our neighbors and with our life as a whole.

Bridging this gap between purposeful being and our selfish self, we as Christians see Jesus as the Christ.

Jesus the Christ responded to the serpent. He did not change the stone into bread. He was not a bread king. He was not a dictator, ruling over his followers by just keeping people content, or by making them slaves and rewarding them with just the necessities. He did not throw himself off the wall to rule with miracles. No trickery. He didn't force people to follow him with indisputable signs of power. People kept their humanity, their freedom.

And on top of the temple, Jesus refused to rule with sheer power, status, or position. He didn't put himself over other people. He didn't bow down to the serpent, and that is why we call him the Christ.

He kept his union with God unbroken — the power and movement of life — pure love.

Adam and Eve — as I said earlier, the story is not ancient history. It is rather meant as personal history, a kind of biography of every person. Adam — humanity; Eve — life, human life.

We corrupt, and we are corrupted. That's the story of Adam and Eve. And that's our story as well; but we are forgiven, loved, and prodded forward by a loving Father. Righteousness is not ours, but his. We know his forgiveness, his love, and his righteousness in Jesus Christ. In him, we are made new people — new people!

21

Christ intensifies the insights of Genesis. Christ says, "All that lies behind you and all the charges laid against you, I have torn to pieces.

"I have nailed the tattered shreds of your life to my cross. Your past simply does not interest me anymore. I am interested only in what I want to make of you, how I can work through you in all aspects of your life."

We can become the media through which God's love can encounter others. It's a matter of fulfillment. It's a matter of life's intention.

In the midst of our daily struggles, we ask help not to compromise our faith, not to be open to the serpent or become the serpent, but to be open for God's guiding presence and life. In Christ, we are made new people. In Christ's name we pray. Amen.

May the peace of God, which passes all understanding, keep our hearts and minds through Christ Jesus. Amen.

Sermon delivered February 12, 1978
Resurrection Lutheran Church
Hamilton Square, New Jersey

Lent 2
Genesis 28:10-17; Mark 8:31-38

Ladders And Towers

*Jacob left Beer-sheba and went toward Haran. He came
to a certain place and stayed there for the night, because the sun had set. Taking one of the stones of the
place, he put it under his head and lay down in that
place. And he dreamed that there was a ladder set up
on the earth, the top of it reaching to heaven; and the
angels of God were ascending and descending on it.
And the Lord stood beside him and said, "I am the Lord,
the God of Abraham your father and the God of Isaac;
the land on which you lie I will give to you and to your
offspring; and your offspring shall be like the dust of
the earth, and you shall spread abroad to the west and
to the east and to the north and to the south; and all the
families of the earth shall be blessed in you and in your
offspring. Know that I am with you and will keep you
wherever you go, and will bring you back to this land;
for I will not leave you until I have done what I have
promised you." Then Jacob woke from his sleep and
said, "Surely the Lord is in this place — and I did not
know it!" And he was afraid, and said, "How awesome
is this place! This is none other than the house of God,
and this is the gate of heaven."* — Genesis 28:10-17

A number of summers ago, my family and I were hiking in the
high desert country of Colorado. We hiked along a cliff trail near
the top of a mesa wall. We could see down into the massive canyon
below us, but we could also see above the other mesas around us. It
was a western sky and it seemed as if you could see forever. As we
hiked, farther and farther way from where we were camped, we
noticed an approaching thunderstorm. With a sight line over the

23

plateau, we could observe the storm enlarge, or at least that is how it appeared, as it drew closer. There was an incredible amount of electrical activity in the heart of the storm; repetitive bolts of lightning flashed through the blackness of the massive thunderhead — a large enveloping anvil cloud. The storm approached at a very impressive rate of speed. The ominous cloud was sweeping toward us. The rest of the sky, which had been sharp blue turned a wispy white, and then seemed to be sucked into the growing thunderhead. The rumble of the thunder soon turned into a distinct explosion of sound. Before the rain struck us, there was a strong blast of wind, gusting thirty to forty, maybe fifty miles per hour, picking up dust and twigs along the ridge trail. It was an awesome and fearful moment. It was a loud rush of wind and we were very vulnerable, high up on the narrow trail. It seemed as though we had been moved into the center of chaos — into a reverse creation as things flew apart. The gunshot — explosive thunder, the force of the wind, the sudden mid-afternoon darkness, and then the rain — a cascade of rain, which quickly overwhelmed the upper mesa floor with water that then came tumbling down on us in the form of waterfalls, water falling down the cliffs onto us and our narrow trail hugging the rock wall.

Now this may all sound very exciting to you, and it was, I assure you; it was for my family at that moment, very terrifying. We hugged the rock wall; everything became very slippery, the water crashing down on the path and then over the edge of the path to fall far down into the valley below. There was almost no visibility. Feeling our way along the wall, and under one of these temporary waterfalls, we were surprised by a small, low, round hole in the rock surface — an entrance to a cave. We entered through the hole in the cave. It was powder dry inside. Peaceful. We hugged each other, stopped crying, and stopped trembling. It was like heaven.

The storm eventually passed by, the wind and rain ending about as quickly as it had started. The waterfalls off the cliffs above turned from torrents into trickles of clear water. The sun emerged, bright and sharp. Everything was fresh and clean outside. We came out of the cave and stood in the warmth of the sun and then continued our hike along the path. It wasn't too far until we came to a location where up above us on the cliff wall was a petroglyph — there were symbols and stick-like pictures made by the Anasazi Indians who lived here below the mesa about a thousand years ago. The path we were walking on was first used by the Anasazi. The petroglyph above, we learned later, was a map, a swirling map supposedly showing where the center of the earth is located. At the center of the earth is a small round hole into the earth. From there, under the guidance of a caring God, all human beings (all the various tribes of people) had emerged into the sunlight. They emerged self-realized, and designed, the Anasazi believed, for loving interaction — designed this way by the creator of all animated life. They emerged from this hole in the earth to live in caring community on the mesa cliffs and beyond. In times of danger, or when caring turned to hate or in war times perhaps, in those times when chaos seemed to rule supreme, there might be safety closer to the creator if one could only return to the center of the earth from which we all emerged created for loving harmony; if one could only decipher the map on the cliff wall and find the way back.

Under the waterfall of the storm of chaos, I believe my family and I had inadvertently found the opening — God's peace under a waterfall of a storm of chaos that was self-formed.

> *Jacob woke up startled, and said, "The Lord is here! God is even in this place, and I didn't know it!" Jacob was afraid and said, "What a terrifying place this is! It must be the house of God; it must be the gate that opens into heaven."*   — Genesis 28:16-17 (paraphrased)

Our first lesson reading this morning from the book of Genesis is a walk on the high desert that projects us back to the dawn of history and beyond — back into the layering of storytelling over centuries, stories that eventually were interwoven and rewritten and codified into our cycle of "Jacob stories." This morning's story of Jacob and the staircase to heaven is perhaps the most important of the series, or at least it is the center point for all the other of the Jacob traditions.

It is also a very serious story because we are all in a sense, personally involved in it. After all, Jacob is our relative (for if we are spiritual sons and daughters of Abraham and Sarah, as the church claims, then Jacob is close family). Jacob is on the move — Jacob the crook, the swindler, the deceiver — Jacob the ungrateful brother and son — Jacob the blasphemer. All that is deceitful in us is right there in Jacob.

I am sure you remember the situation that led up to today's story. After tricking Esau, his brother, out of his rightful birthright, after deceiving his blind father who was lying on his deathbed, and after stealing the family fortune, Jacob was making tracks out of town. He had left on the run and he didn't stop until it was dark and supposedly safe because there he could hide in the darkness. Only then did Jacob lay down to sleep, but alone in the dark shadows of that night, he had a dream.

Dreams in that ancient time held much power because, it was believed, they revealed something true. A dream had the power to peel back the curtains of mystery to reveal final truth.

Jacob dreamed that there was a staircase set up on the earth, and the top of the steps reached to heaven; and behold, angels of God were ascending and descending on it. (Remember that at that time angels were perceived not as winged, sexless chubby cupids, but rather as serious messengers, envoys who would surprise us by bringing us into direct contact with God — the very word of God personalized.)

Envoys were ascending and descending the steps; and then Jacob, according to the text, saw God, Yahweh, standing at the head of the steps who proclaimed,

> *I am the Lord, the God of Abraham and Sarah, and the God of Isaac and Abraham — the God of all that should matter to you. I, God, offer to you a future and a place to live in close human relationships. Behold, I offer you a blessing. I, God, will be with you, and will keep you wherever you go!*
>
> — Genesis 28:13-15 (paraphrased)

26

Jacob awoke from his sleep, startled, and he stammered,
"Surely the Lord is in this place, and I did not know it."
Jacob, in fear and trembling, said, "How awesome is
this place! This is none other than Bethel — Beth-El,
the house of God — this is the very Gate of Heaven!"
— Genesis 28:16-17 (paraphrased)

There are some things happening in this text that we must be honest about. There was an ancient Canaanite sanctuary, a temple community, that was viewed as the house of Canaanite gods. It was near this site where Jacob rested for the night. What the story does is to legitimatize Yahweh-worship at the pre-Israelite cultic center of Bethel. After all, an Israelite patriarch, Jacob, has now proclaimed that this place is also sacred to Yahweh. Yahweh is top power. The idea of specific location, which was very important to the priests of Yahweh misses, I believe, the revelation, or blessing, of the Jacob's ladder story. Jacob did not stay at Bethel, but God kept the promise to be with Jacob wherever he went.

A quick word about some of the imagery in this story. Staircases extending into heaven, that pierce the boundary between the human and God, were in the visions and traditions of a number of different, ancient peoples. My favorite tradition of this type is contained in a poem about Nut, the Egyptian sky goddess and mother of Osiris. The sky goddess arches her naked, athletic body over the earth's flat surface to form the sky barrier between earth and heaven, the human and the divine. But according to the poem, if one could discover the location of her feet, where her feet touch the ground, as the poem put it, "then her back a ladder is, its vertebrae the rungs" to climb into the divine, like the Anasazi's hole into the center of the earth.

People have always tried to put their most important symbolism into physical form. The Anasazi Indians built subterranean, circular rooms — kivas — with a small opening at ground level, and a ladder leading down into the earthen room. They would enter back into the ground to be regenerated in the kiva, to smoke together while fires heated water into steam. They would be enveloped by the presence of God in the earth, and in the kiva they could best tell the ancient oral traditions of their origin and of the creator's desire for their well-being and harmony when they left the cave at the center of the earth. The particular imagery of Jacob's staircase was expressed at that time in Babylonian Ziggurats, step-tower temples such as the famous Marduk temple of Babylon in present-day Iraq — a little southwest of Baghdad on a branch of the Euphrates. One approaches the god in the upper temple chamber by ascending a massive, steep staircase. The same image was picked up by the grand staircase in the royal palaces of the regional kings in the ancient Near East. The angels coming and going were like the messengers and emissaries of the earthly kings who after all were supposed to represent God.

Remember that just a few chapters before, in the book of Genesis, was the story of the tower of Babel. The staircase of that tower was a human attempt to build what Jacob had experienced in his dream. The difference was that in Babel, we were attempting to build the ladder; it was to be established on our terms and where we wanted it. The tower was for us.

Theologically the Jacob story was radically different. The staircase — the divine connection — was God's action, a gift, God's blessing to be with you wherever you go: "I will not leave you. I will always offer you my love."

We build our tower-temples today — the Trump Tower in Manhattan, for example, is pink marble and polished brass and glass on Fifth Avenue. On the lower lever, one is greeted by a waterfall and a massive, shining moving staircase, a silver escalator ascending and descending, leading to and coming from the heavens above. The staircase leads up to various levels where there are the most chic and glamorous boutiques and shops that our consumer culture can offer. Higher still, top office spaces at rent levels that factor out all but those who are at the very pinnacle of the corporate ladder; and up in the clouds of the Trump Tower is the penthouse abode of our gods and goddesses of power and wealth and prestige. Chicago's "Magnificent Mile," along North Michigan Avenue added another such tower-temple to that city's skyscape — "Chicago Place" — gateway to consumer heaven.

We build towers to honor or please ourselves, but that is Babel and not Bethel, and I am interested this morning in Bethel — the map to the house of God.

One of the first cosmonauts placed in orbit by the Soviet Union reported from space that he was now in the heavens — he had climbed the staircase — and he didn't see any God, so there must be no God.

Russell (Rusty) Schweickart, I remember, was a smart, quiet, red-headed child who was an acolyte at my dad's church in New Jersey. He went to Massachusetts Institute of Technology and was a quiet honor student; but later, he, too, was blasted into space. He became an Apollo astronaut and was the first human being to ever float free in space, alone, without an umbilical cord life-support system. It was all self-contained in his backpack.

His story is rather routine up to that particular moment. Before the flight, he remembers meetings upon meetings, going over procedures and detailed checklists, simulations of everything that could happen or go wrong, hours in the classroom struggling to keep awake, and an infinite series of physical examinations. Ascending the staircase into the rocket and even the lift off was, he said, rather anticlimactic. Watching from the beach, it's very exciting — all smoke and fire and power — but inside the space craft, everything looked and felt very much as it did in the simulations that he had done a hundred times before, except now everything worked correctly. He ascended about as high as most humans have ever ascended (though "ascension" and even descriptions of height and depth lose most of their meaning in space). Eventually it came time for him to walk in space — to drift alone. At first he was kept busy checking dials and gauges, but then a camera jammed in the command module, and they told him to relax and do nothing while they tried to fix the camera. So he floated out there, in space, and he looked around and stared at the earth and saw it anew. He said later, "I saw the continent of Africa and it was home; it was my home. And then India, then Burma and Southeast Asia, and it was all home, all its music and poetry and art and love and tears and joy."

His walk in space occurred during the time of one of the Arab-Israeli wars; people were killing each other in a desert below. Rusty wrote later, "You look down there and you can't imagine how many borders and boundaries you cross, again and again and again, and you don't even see them. There you are, and hundreds of people in the Middle East are killing each other over some imaginary line that you're not even aware of, that you can't even see. The world is a whole, and it's beautiful, and you wish you could take one person in each hand, one from each side in the various global conflicts, and say, 'Look! Look at it from this perspective. Look at what's important.'"

It is a bit like old sinful Jacob before the staircase. Rusty said later, "Am I separated out to be touched by God, to have some special experience that others cannot have? There's nothing that I've done that deserves that, that earned that. We are to be a sensing element for all humanity. You look down and see the surface of that globe that you've lived on all this time, and you know all those people down there, and they are like you — they are you — somehow you represent them. You now have a responsibility, and it's not for yourself. You are out there on that forefront. And you have to bring that back somehow. It's a special responsibility, and it tells you something about your relationship with this thing we call life — something new. When I came back there was a difference in that world. There's a difference in that relationship between you and that planet and you and all these other forms of life on that planet, and it's so precious."

Rusty called it an encounter with the will of God, and has now dedicated his life to environmental concerns and to the peace movement. (There are ways to bring about justice and stability without killing people in the desert.)

> *Jacob woke up and said, "The Lord is here! God is in this place, and I didn't know it. This must be the house of God; it must be the gate that opens into heaven."*
> — Genesis 28:16 (paraphrased)

Right here Genesis overlaps our gospel reading — the disciples walking a dusty road on a journey that will lead to Jerusalem and a cross.

> *If any want to become my followers, let them deny themselves and take up their cross and follow me.*
> — Mark 8:34

The confession of the church was that right there, on the road together, was God, walking with them, the Christ present in any location. Here is Bethel! *"God is in this place, and I didn't know it"* is the confession of the disciples after the crucifixion. *"God still here with us"* is the Easter morning confession. Here is the center of the earth offered wherever you may be — the end of the storm, the source of peace, of safety, and of responsibility to others in need of peace and safety, all called into servanthood.

> *Jacob dreamed that he saw a stairway reaching from earth to heaven, and there was the Lord standing before him. "I am the Lord, the God of Abraham and Isaac, I will be with you and protect you wherever you go. I will not leave you. I desire to bless you now, here, always — and bless others through you."*
> — Genesis 28:12-13 (paraphrased)

Sermon delivered February 24, 1991
Weaver Chapel
Wittenberg University
Springfield, Ohio

A Letter From Cousin John

Rabbi, who sinned, this man or his parents, that he was born blind?   — John 9:2b

Some of those who were with Jesus heard about his effect on people — about those being brought into wholeness — the dead raised, the hungry fed, the blind given sight. And they said to Jesus, "Surely we are not also blind, are we?"
                              — John 9:40 (paraphrased summary)

For once you were in darkness ... Sleeper, awake! Rise from the dead....   — Ephesians 5:8, 14

... though I walk through the valley of the shadow of death....   — Psalm 23:4 (RSV)

Did you ever receive a letter from a dead person? I did once. My cousin, John, sent me such a letter. I only had two cousins — John and Connie.

John was an honors student at Franklin and Marshall College when, during his senior year, he decided to pack-it-all-in and leave school, do a little farming in New Hampshire, and make candles to sell.

It was the early 1970s and John had had enough of a world apparently perched on the edge of chaos — what with the Cold War threatening nuclear annihilation; with young people his own age being shot at Kent State, and shooting and being shot in Vietnam.

John drifted to San Francisco and put some of his artistic talent into making stained-glass windows. He scared himself when he became in great demand — the big hotels wanting his art-deco glasswork at any price. But John wanted meaning, not money; he wanted clear vision, not a fat bank account.

So Cousin John moved on and wandered through Zimbabwe, Angola, and Mozambique, for years, crossing borders on foot late at night, his very white skin and very red hair a distinct novelty.

John was a pacifist. Unarmed, traveling alone, dealing in antique ivory and butterfly wings, he was often stopped by bandits and occasionally by various revolutionary forces who would thrust a rifle barrel to his head, their eyes revealing a ready will to end this alien life in their midst.

> ... *though I walk through the valley of the shadow of death....*   — Psalm 23:4 (RSV)

But John would always smile and talk them out of killing him. He had a gift of negotiation and identification and he always seemed to know enough of the right tribal language.

And there was, I am sure, a certain rush, after all, a grand thrill from such life-threatening encounters that no college philosophy class or San Francisco drug scene could match.

> *Rabbi, who sinned, this man or his parents, that he was born blind?*   — John 9:2b

One day while standing on the veranda of an old victorian-British-empire-era hotel in Nairobi and drinking Tusker Beer, Cousin John was offered the job of organizing oil exploration camps in remote areas of the Sudan. John had such a fine rapport with indigenous laborers. John never seemed to me to have even an ounce of racial prejudice within him, and it was obvious to others.

But John soon became rich again, and so he ran again and ended up in Scotland putting slate roofs on old castles. It was there and then that the gnawing at his soul reached a peak. What really is the meaning of it all, of all of life? Riches and drugs and the exotic and success — there must be something that certainly and finally transcends these all.

His will for peace, for racial and global harmony, for equality and inner equilibrium combined then with a realization of a very real God, outside the human will for good. This is the realization of a very real God with a force that is very personal, not just something that we humans patch together, but God as an independent will — real and active and offering that harmony and peace for which John searched the world, including the inner realm of his own soul.

Sleeper; awake! Rise from the dead....
— Ephesians 5:14

Well, John came home in more ways than one. He physically returned to the States and made contact with his family, but also he came home with a vision of Jesus — of God alive and caring.

Always a generous person, John combined his skills and dreams for such things as solar energy and other alternate energy sources, preserving the good earth, along with his sensitivity to the great needs of the Third World. John started the Southern Slate Company in Atlanta, a construction and roofing business that quickly earned a reputation for high artistic quality, the best materials, and low prices. He specialized in church roofs.

And John purposely hired the hard-core unemployed from inner-city Atlanta — unskilled laborers, teaching them the art of slating — "giving them pride, skills, and a future" is what John firmly believed.

And then John met a young woman, and they made marriage commitments to each other, forever. He wrote in that letter to me, his cousin, "[Marriage] is a big step for me and it feels absolutely perfect in terms of the overall parade of events in my life."

John wrote to me to share his joy, his new inner peace and faith, and purposeful future, and to tell me that he wanted me to be at his wedding. He mailed the letter to me on a warm, Georgia day in November, but before I received the letter, John was murdered. Robbed and murdered in his own modest apartment. The killer has

35

not been identified. Police speculate that it was an unemployed drifter who had heard of John's hospitality and had set up a phony job interview at John's place.

My cousin, John. What is all this? Just another statistic of urban crime and violence? Just one of the thousands of murders each year in this country?

We all have to die, but my dear cousin, John? So much loving potential, finally finding a hopeful future combining vocation and love. Is this the reward for his search and his newfound peace? My cousin, John. We were just beginning to be able to talk again. We actually did, in Atlanta, just a few months before the letter, and I wanted so much to become close to him again, as close as we were in those pre-teen years when we used to have pillow fights together and play miniature golf late into the hot, lazy evenings on the boardwalk when his family would make their annual summer visit to the shore. And now John is dead.

In the light of the big picture, does it really make any difference at all? We do live in a Lenten world that holds betrayal and crucifixion. Not only physical death, but also, often, pure injustice, whether shot on the Zimbabwe border, or murdered in Atlanta in the prime of life, or finished off by cancer at age 85 — every smile and embrace and mistake made in the brief moments of our life before death.... Did it take my dear cousin's murder to drive this reality home to me — to my sense of safety and hope?

> *... though I walk through the shadow of death....*
> — Psalm 23:4 (RSV)

How does that psalm continue?

We can all dig out letters, buried away in desk or bureau drawers at home, letters written by beloved family members now long gone; and I am not viewing this as some idealized cycle of nature renewing itself — good death, but rather as death snatching my dear letter-writing cousin away, and eventually all our cousins — dying when steel displaces flesh in violence in Atlanta, or when the body begins to consume itself during days of starvation in the

Sudan, or just the human body wearing down after a near century of animation, or any other human ending.

"Here is the astonishing thing! You do not know where he comes from, and yet he opened my eyes," said the one who was once blind but now can see. He is talking to us, to our culture, reminding us Christians.

> *For once you were darkness, but now in the Lord you are light. Live as children of light — for the fruit of the light is found in all that is good and right and true.*
> *— Ephesians 5:8-9*

John had come home and is still at home.

There is a tomb gateway to an Easter answer that even now, this fourth Sunday in Lent, in the Lenten season of our lives, even now, there is an Easter answer that whispers, "Yes."

Lent takes us into the reality of suffering and separation but never out of sight of Easter light. It is all according to our gospel text a new way of looking at things that has nothing to do with cones and rods. It is being in the light of God. There is a certainty and continuity in God's personal love and forgiveness. My dear cousin was forging a life for others that was imaging the model of Christ — and was therefore from God — and God is eternal.

> *Sleeper, awake! Rise from the dead, and Christ will shine on you.* *— Ephesians 5:14*

> *... though I walk through the valley of the shadow of death, I shall fear no evil; for you — God — are with me ... surely your goodness and mercy shall follow me all the days of my life, and I will dwell in the house of the Lord forever.* *— Psalm 23:4, 6 (paraphrased)*

Sermon delivered March 17, 1996
Weaver Chapel
Wittenberg University
Springfield, Ohio

37

Lent 5
John 12:20-33

New York Cathedrals

> *Now among those who went up to worship at the festival were some Greeks. They came to Philip, who was from Bethsaida in Galilee, and said to him, "Sir we wish to see Jesus." Philip went and told Andrew; then Andrew and Philip went and told Jesus. Jesus answered them, "The hour has come for the Son of Man to be glorified. Very truly, I tell you, unless a grain of wheat falls into the earth and dies, it remains just a single grain; but if it dies, it bears much fruit. Those who love their life will lose it, and those who hate their life in this world will keep it for eternal life. Whoever serves me must follow me, and where I am, there will my servant be also. Whoever serves me, the Father will honor."*
> — John 12:20-26

According to today's assigned gospel reading, there were some Greeks who approached the students and followers of Jesus and said, "We want to see Jesus." Who were these Greeks?

This is a pivotal section of the book of John, located right in the center of its story. Some Greeks appear, wanting to see Jesus. They were not Palestinian Jews; they were not extended clan or local neighbors from Galilee, or Samaritans, or religious leaders from Jerusalem, or Roman police, or local spies whose business it was to keep an eye on anyone who gathered a crowd. Who were these Greeks who approached the disciples with the request, "We want to see Jesus"?

What we know about these Greeks is that they were people from the outside looking in. They may or may not have been Jews, but being Greek-speaking and probably from way north, set them apart. They were outsiders who didn't know much about Jesus — perhaps just some vague claims that they had heard, that Jesus offered clear insight into what God desires for us. And so these curious Greeks had a question for the disciples. "We have heard some things about your Jesus, and now we want to see for ourselves."

What follows in the text is a confession, a summary of the big picture about Jesus' life and his death and his resurrection. It's a "faith statement." It is the Christian claim that the sacrificial, self-giving life of Jesus reveals in all its purity God's hope and future for us all.

This story about those inquisitive Greeks is at the center of John's gospel because the faith community of John was located, not in Jerusalem or Palestine, but in the midst of the Greek-speaking world. This congregation was at the crossroads of multiple traditions and cultures. This section of the story says to the diverse mix of Greek-speaking seekers on the outside of the church that this message about Jesus is for them also. You all are to be included.

This part of the book is also reminding the members of the congregation that the life and message about Jesus is transcultural; it is for all people, it transcends even religion. It is about God wanting to love, affirm, and engage everyone. And each member of John's congregation had the responsibility to spread that word. Jesus said, "I draw [all people] to myself."

And so, according to the text, there were Greeks who came to a worship festival, Greeks bearing a request of the disciples, "We want to see this Jesus of yours."

I had an opportunity a week ago to use some vacation days to visit my parents and my two brothers and their families. I am from a rather small family, but now some of my nieces and my nephews' spouses are having babies, and when we gathered for my dad's 79th birthday party, there must have been about twenty Wuchters there. That's about all of us. With all the little children, it was an energetic reunion.

And I hate to tell you this, but it is spring in New Jersey. The grass is green. There is even the sound of lawn mowers in the air.

The daffodils are ending their glorious reign, but the tulips are poised to take over. The flowering trees are stunning, including some magnolias and ornamental cherries. Just about every yard is awash in yellow forsythia.

My daughter, Kirsten, and her husband, Bob, drove from Michigan to join us. Bob is unfamiliar with the area so we took him on a tour. Wednesday we went into Manhattan for the day. In Central Park, all the trees had golden buds and newly unfolded leaves, including the lacy weeping willows by the ponds. Songbirds were singing their little hearts out, marking territory, attracting mates, or carrying bits of grass or yarn in their beaks to finish off nests.

We purchased some half-price theater tickets at the booth on Times Square and then went for a walk before lunch and a two o'clock matinee. We watched the skaters at Rockefeller Center and then decided to show Bob the two grand cathedrals that stand side-by-side on Fifth Avenue. We went first into St. Patrick's Cathedral. The first worship held there after its completion was in May, 121 years ago, in 1879. At that time, St. Patrick's dominated its space on Fifth Avenue, but now, of course, it finds itself in the shadows of the surrounding skyscrapers. For me, at least, there is still a sense of the sacred in that space in the middle of the bustling city. It is quiet inside, for one thing, and, of course, the high arching ceilings force you to look up and beyond yourself. It's important to look beyond yourself in today's world.

St. Pat's is also filled with the clutter of ancient symbolism. One has the feeling that things haven't changed much in 121 years. Oh sure, there are now closed-circuit television screens on the back of each pillar so if you are stuck behind one on Christmas Eve or at a mid-morning mass on Easter Day, or at a celebrity funeral (about the only times the church there is really filled for worship anymore!), you can still see the chancel and pulpit on the screen. But the rest of what surrounds you, the side altars, sculptures, paintings, and stained glass, are in the European Gothic style from centuries past: pious saints, Jesus on the cross, a Pieta or two — Jesus dead in the arms of Mary, and symbolic images of an empty tomb.

There were two kinds of people in St. Patrick's that spring day. Both groups were composed of people of various ages, races, and cultural backgrounds — that's not what divided them. Those in the much smaller of the two groupings could be found kneeling by the side altars, or sitting up in the very front pews before the main altar at the center of the transept. These people were deep into prayer or meditation or confession. Their body language and detachment from what was all around them at that moment indicated to me a genuine, spiritual relationship with God, or at least a deep desire for some transcendent forgiveness, or acceptance, or divine guidance.

The other category of people in the cathedral that day formed the vast majority. It was all the people who were politely milling around, silently looking everywhere, and walking up and down the aisles; tourists with cameras in hand, office workers on lunch or coffee break, street people, and a school group on tour. These were the people that I watched most closely. Many, I am sure, were people of great faith in God and active in their own worship communities. But many, I believe, were not. Most in this group seemed to possess something more than just curiosity. I perceived in most a sense of wonder — perhaps also an experience of solitude, and a respectful interest in the imagery that surrounded them. I believe it was more than a "museum-like curiosity"; after all, they had to look over members of that other group, those disciples, who were deep in prayer or thought before the statue next to the ornate altar and the glowing votive candles.

For some, I am sure, it was a sense of wonder. They wondered about the meaning that others have found in that wood carving of Jesus hanging on a cross above that white marble altar, or in Jesus reaching out to children in a painting, or in that surreal icon of Jesus pictured with a halo and being lifted into a baroque sky of white billowing clouds. What does all this mean? What can it mean for us today?

I believe that many of those people in the pensive majority that day, slowly walking through the cathedral, are the Greeks of our text today. They are contemporary truth seekers looking for some kind of grounded meaning. I could almost hear them whisper, "We, too, want to see this Jesus. I wonder if he has any meaning outside of this massive building filled with candle smoke and ancient images? Does Jesus have any peace to offer me in my chaotic, and, I am afraid, random life"?

Do you know any of these Greek seekers from work or school or your neighborhood?

We then took Bob to the other massive cathedral of worship that is right next door — Saks Fifth Avenue. Here, the pace was more upbeat, more hurried, the sounds more contemporary, and the place was more crowded. For spring and the Easter shopping season, Saks is now decorated with massive tree branches. They were artificial, of course, but tall branches topped with spring green leaf buds were placed in each aisle along the columns of the main floor. And the branches were arranged to form high arches, reminiscent of St. Patrick's. Shoppers and gawkers walk down the aisles under these beautiful arches to enter into the main chancel area, which at Saks is the extensive beauty aids department. Here at the center of things, are row upon row of polished wood and glass altars that hold eye shadow and perfume and lip gloss, each altar attended by a priestess in a white lab coat, each representing one of the various gods or goddesses of the beauty pantheon: Yves Saint Laurent, Liz Claiborne, Ralph Lauren, Calvin Klein, and Gucci — individual priestesses in white robes wanting you to sit down in their little confessional booths before the mirror where you can confess how you are not as pretty, or as attractive as you would like to be, confessing, "There are too many wrinkles; I want to look younger" or "My hair is all wrong" or "Would a different lip color make me sexier, more desirable?" Help me, beauty priestess!

On the altars next to the mirrors throughout the store are large, clear, glass vases filled with freshly cut, waxy, white calla lilies, and pedestals holding blooming, white orchid plants. There is a constant offering being taken in this sanctuary, as people flash VISA gold and Master Card platinum.

But there wasn't much solitude in this cathedral, and the clergy in the while coats seemed a little desperate. I think that they are on commission. Can you really trust their compliments and their recommendations? In fact, many of the seekers of beauty and acceptance in Saks seemed to me to be a bit desperate, too. "How long can I cover up what I really am?" "I want to be beautiful but not phony. Can I get that here?" "I want to be loved for what I really am." "Help me!"

It seemed to me that there were a lot of Greeks in Saks Fifth Avenue last week — a lot of Greeks at the worship festival in that cathedral desiring more permanent answers. Though they were certainly not naming the name of Jesus, I believe that many were asking in the depths of their souls to see the Messiah, to encounter the peace of God.

Do you know any of these Greeks in your schools, clubs, work place, or play place?

According to today's gospel text, these Greeks came to the festival, sought out the disciples of Jesus, and asked the disciples to take them to Jesus. Well, the Greeks are still with us, but who are the disciples today?

We are! And that's what you confirmands are confessing to be today: disciples of Jesus. That's what you told me you were in the faith statements that you wrote this month. You are the disciples of Jesus today. Well, are you ready to take the Greeks to Jesus?

Not that you have all the answers for them or even for yourself. Faith, after all, is not knowing about God but having a relationship with God. It is alive; it is dynamic. It is beyond mere facts and figures. Martin Luther said faith is the "yes of the heart" on which we stake our lives.

And you have a lot to share with these contemporary Greeks. Today you are affirming your baptism. Confirmation day is another opportunity, in the vast string of opportunities that form your life, to say to God, "Yes, if it is thy will!" "Yes, Jesus loves me!" As smart, talented young adults you are called to move beyond the childhood concepts that held meaning for you when you were younger, non-abstract thinkers, but now is the time to claim a nurturing relationship with God as your own. Not just something passed down or borrowed, but now as a part of who you are. We want you to move from a belief structure that you received from family or church to a living faith that you own, and therefore can share with the Greeks — with all the seekers of truth and meaning that you will continue to encounter.

In a sense, as an adult member of this congregation, we want to you to participate in our shared religious life because you want to. We want you to discern the reality and action of God even in the ambiguities of life and death. We don't want you to avoid uncomfortable questions, or move into some sort of fundamentalism where you regard faith as absolute answers instead of a living relationship. We want this relationship with God to be at the core of your personal identity, first for your own well-being and peace, but also so you can bring this wholeness to all those who come to you saying that they too want to see Jesus.

There is so much to share with these Greeks who seek meaning! And you can do it! You can tell them, and show them, for example, the sacred nature of God's good creation, and the sisterhood and brotherhood of all humanity. Help them to understand and respect the differences of culture, race, and history, and to know that such human diversity should not lead to divisions but to a celebration of unity, of one neighborhood, of one family.

Show them through your decisions and actions how to tell the difference between good and evil so that they can make a loving difference in the lives of others. Help them not to be bullied or belittled by trends or fads or by the threats of society, or by peer pressure to be less than they were intended to be. Help them to see Jesus by showing respect and compassion for the oppressed and marginalized in our global society, by living your own life in ways that do not overlook the sick, the hungry, the homeless, the distraught, or those in despair. You can help others to see Jesus and the long reach of God's love that stretches even beyond the tomb.

The whole time that you have been a member of First Lutheran Church, you have been a valued and equal member of our community, blessed by God, but on your confirmation day, you are welcomed into the full responsibility of a disciple of Jesus. And that includes speaking to, and reaching out to, the Greeks around you. Under the forgiveness and loving acceptance of God, you are to live that confession of faith that you endorse.

45

"Now among those who went up to worship at the festival were some Greeks. They came to the disciples of Jesus, and said, "We wish to see Jesus."

May they see Jesus in and through you. Amen.

Sermon delivered April 9, 2000
First Lutheran Church
Duluth, Minnesota

Passion/Palm Sunday
Matthew 21:1-11; 26:14—27:66

Parade

*Tell the city of Zion: Look, your king is coming to you,
he is humble, and rides on a donkey and on a colt, the
foal of a donkey.*   — Zechariah 9:9 (paraphrased)

Jesus enters Jerusalem. The parade begins.

*A great crowd of people spread their cloaks on the road,
while others cut branches from the trees and spread
them on the road. The crowds walking in front of Jesus
and the crowds walking behind began to shout: "Praise
to David's son; God bless him who comes in the name
of the Lord! Praise be to God. Hosanna."*
                         — Matthew 21:8-9 (paraphrased)

Palm Sunday is also known in the church calendar as the Sunday of the Passion. Alternate gospel readings for the day continue
the story. Reading a few chapters later in Matthew, a few days after
the parade:

*"What then shall I do with Jesus called the Christ?"
Pilate asked the crowd. "Nail him to the cross," they
all answered. But Pilate asked, "What crime has he
committed?" They started shouting at the top of their
voices, "Nail him to the cross." Then Pilate set Barabbas
free for them; he had Jesus whipped and then handed
him over to be nailed to the cross. Pilate's soldiers took
Jesus, stripped off his clothes and put a scarlet robe on
him. They made a crown out of thorny branches and
put it on this head, and made fun of him. They spit on*

him and took a stick and beat him over the head. When they finished making fun of him, they took the robe off and put his own clothes on him and then led him out to nail him to the cross. They nailed him to the cross and then divided his clothes among themselves by throwing dice. People passing by shook their heads and threw insults at Jesus. Even the bandits who had been crucified with him insulted him in the same way.

— Matthew 27:22-44 (paraphrased)

From "Hosanna!" to "Crucify him!" From a parade to an execution. From palms to passion. From celebration to rejection. Jesus enters Jerusalem. It seems like a parade. People following before and after, waving flags like branches, laying not confetti but colored cloth before the participants — cheering — excitement — celebration — holiday mood.

As the total picture begins to develop, this was not an ordinary parade; in fact, it was sort of the reverse — the opposite of a normal parade.

Think about parades.

Since humanity first became stable enough to do some farming and cluster dwellings together to form villages, there have been parades. The first parades were the movements of troops — soldiers moving from one strategic position to another, marching through a town. It was a necessary movement but also a show of strength and power and control. Troops that could move through a town in an orderly fashion without looting it were a cause for celebration. A sign for protection.

Trumpets called attention to this movement of power. Drums kept marching time, and then other instruments all added to the sense of excitement.

When the leaders of a country or dynasty would move about their land, they would travel in the company of troops for protection and as signs of power. Their flags and banners and horses and chariots or coaches would be the best possible, the most expensive, the flashiest, to call attention to their power and class.

48

Such excursions or parades were something to see even if you didn't particularly like the leaders who passed by on their white horses or open chariots — like our politicians waving from polished convertibles.

Thousands of years ago these parades were occurring daily around the globe. African chieftains in all their splendor were being carried through tribal empires, chariot after chariot; and hundreds of armed horsemen were moving through the delicate villages of eastern China, dynasty after dynasty.

The slapping of sandals on stone pavements, the flashing of swords and armor as Roman soldiers marched through the Northern Mediterranean, and Near East and Europe: parades to show off the newest weapons, to elicit cheers, respect and fear, to show the power to those in control. Some of the best examples of this kind of parade today are the May Day parades in the Eastern European countries — a time to march the troops, put up the banners, and show off the newest weapons, rocket-launching tanks, and anti-missile-missiles — signs of power, wealth, control.

And Jesus rode into Jerusalem on a donkey.

Some parades also elicit fear. This is the power of war and death held in the hands of these marching men. It's the power to destroy that is coiled up in those weapons and sinews.

The best example of fear at a parade that I witnessed was in Greece a few years ago. A crisis on Cyprus had brought Greece and Turkey to the brink of an all out war. In a small village I watched an impromptu parade as a ragtag group of called-up men and boys marched through the town, off to prepare for war.

Their uniforms didn't fit. One fellow's helmet fell off as he marched; they looked uncomfortable with their rifles, but it was a parade and the villagers turned out to watch. It was a parade to display power but the aspect of fear dominated and there were more tears than cheers from the solemn audience.

It reminded me of a Greek vase I once saw in a museum that pictured Spartan soldiers marching off to war. They all had swords, helmets, shields, and a look of confidence. They also carried a small bag with one day's supply of food. They were going to battle and tomorrow they would either be home for dinner or be dead.

Also on the vase were the wives waving as the parade marched by — the women were pictured with a tear in each eye, dressed in black. Fear and death — a sign of some parades.

Jesus rode toward death but also toward Easter life.

One other kind of parade that I guess we are most familiar with today is not really a sign of fear or power but is simply an escape from reality — a change of pace — something different to break up the monotony of day-to-day routine. These parades signal a holiday from the normal day, an excuse to get outside and celebrate.

Holiday means holy day, but the religious connection to the day is soon forgotten in the parade and probably was just an excuse to have a parade in the first place. I remember seeing an Assumption Day parade in a little village in France. I don't think anybody knew that it was a holy day; they were just out for a good time. Everybody in the parade was dressed up in bizarre outfits dancing around as those watching cheered. Every once in a while, the parade would stop and the back row of the band would put their instruments down on the street and people would jump off and run into the nearest tavern for a quick glass of wine — joy and escape.

Another example is the pre-Lenten Mardi Gras parade — celebration and escape from reality. Whether in New Orleans or out in Cajun country, the parades are an escape from the every day. While they last they are for sheer enjoyment. Like it is for most of the early marchers in the day-long Mummers Day parade on New Year's Day in Philadelphia, it is a two-day wild orgy of escape from life in South Philly.

One of the wildest parades I ever saw was the Frontier Days parade in Cheyenne, Wyoming. The parade was one big party. Everyone, it seemed, whether in the parade or standing watching, had a can of Coors in one hand and a gun in the other. The people would periodically shoot off their guns into the sky along with a cowboy yell.

The local Lutheran church was even represented in the parade. A large number of church members rode their horses in a group, and they had a float with a big sign on it. On the front of the sign was the name of the church, and on the back, it read in big letters, "God Loves A Good Rodeo."

All parades — celebration and escape, fear and death, power and superiority — many parades combine the themes.

Our local Memorial Day parade is a good example. Memorial Day parades were once a time for armies to march to show military precision and equipment — also to honor and remember those who died in wars past and to show we are ready and prepared to fight and die again if needed. Remnants of that remain. But as the thought of war becomes more removed, Memorial Day parades become more rites of spring, a time to get outside as the June sun and summer approaches, a celebration and escape from winter work.

But there are still signs of competition and power struggle: Which fire company has the most trucks? Which rescue squad has the newest equipment? Which scout troop has the most members? Which baseball team has the classiest uniform?

Parades are signs of power and competition.

And Jesus rides into Jerusalem on a donkey.

Parades are signs of celebration and escape from reality. Jesus rides into Jerusalem and casts the moneychangers out of the temple and teaches and is arrested and executed. Reality, not escape.

Parades are signs of fear and death.

And Jesus rides toward resurrection.

The Palm Sunday story tells of a different kind of parade — a reversal of the status quo. Jesus turns things around. The Palm Sunday parade is not a show of power but a sign of humility and sacrifice. It was not an escape from reality but a movement into reality. Jesus is offering not just a holiday guideline but a direction for every day.

Things are changed around. Jesus is moving toward Jerusalem, moving toward change. This is a different kind of parade that we are watching. Cheers turn to jeers, from "Hosanna" to "Crucify him"; the parade route leads to an execution. Palms to passion — celebration to rejection — it was a parade that showed not the power of weapons but the power of love, not an escape from reality but a movement into the real truth of life in resurrection.

Put yourself into the crowd of the Palm Sunday parade. Do we hail Lord Jesus as our king with palm branches but not always see him in the poor or hungry or the oppressed and the depressed around us? Do we welcome the Prince of Peace into our hearts but warn him to stay out of our business world, out of our politics, out of our prejudices, out of our family budgets, out of our real life? Are we asking him to parade only on holidays like Sunday morning only? Do we greet the King of kings with cheers of hosannas and joy because we have plans for his power but then reject him when we discover that he has plans for our power?

Palm Sunday — the crowds are cheering and waving palms. The Roman soldiers are on alert. The religious establishment is scared, Jesus is riding into Jerusalem!

His last week on earth, the tremendous final drama of his life, is now beginning. Will we, like the crowds, welcome him as king and then turn against him when he begins to change us? Will we compromise his command for love? We ask help that our movement and purpose and personal parade will lead toward Easter life. In Christ's name we pray. Amen.

Sermon delivered March 19, 1978
Resurrection Lutheran Church
Hamilton Square, New Jersey

Maundy Thursday
John 13:1-17, 31b-35

First Communion Class

I give you a new commandment, that you love one an-
other. Just as I have loved you, you also should love
one another.   — John 13:34

It is Thursday in Holy Week. It is the day we remember the last meal Jesus had with his disciples before his execution — Maundy Thursday. "Maundy" from the Latin *Mandatum* that means "command." In the gospel reading from Saint John, Jesus gets up in the middle of the meal and kneels down to wash the feet of his followers. And then this command — *mandatum*:

Just as I have loved you, you also should love one an-
other. By this everyone will know that you are my dis-
ciples, if you have love for one another.
      — John 13:34-35 cf

In the story of the last meal as recorded in the other gospel texts, that same sacrificial servant love is expressed in a different form.

Jesus took the bread and the wine that was a part of the
meal they were sharing, and gave this mandatum: *"Take*
and eat, take and drink, this is my body given for you;
this is my blood shed for you and for all people for the
forgiveness of sin. Do this in remembrance of me."
      — Matthew 26:26-29 (paraphrased)

Maundy Thursday signifies the night of the last supper — the meal in which God breaks into our lives. It is very appropriate that

53

a number of the members of our congregation will be receiving the bread and wine of communion for the first time. Many fifth graders have been in retreat today, along with their parents, preparing for today's opportunity to receive their first communion.

In the first parish I served as pastor, I was the one who taught those classes of preparation. Two weeks ago, I returned to that congregation for a banquet meal as they celebrated their fortieth anniversary as a congregation. They had invited back all their previous pastors. And a few of the members of my first communion classes were there for the anniversary dinner. Those children were now in their late twenties and early thirties, and some had their own children now. I was introduced as "their old pastor," but the memories did flood back. I even dug out some of my old notes from those first classes with fifth graders, when we studied together the mysteries of holy communion.

One of the things we did was to study the words of Martin Luther in his *Small Catechism*: "What benefits do we receive from this sacrament?" Luther asked and then answered, "The benefits of this sacrament are pointed out by the words, 'given and shed for you for the remission of sins.' These words assure us that in the sacrament we receive forgiveness of sin, life, and salvation. For where there is forgiveness of sins, there is also life and salvation. How can eating and drinking do all this? It is not eating and drinking that does this, but the words, 'given and shed for you for the remission of sins.' These words, along with eating and drinking, are the main part of the sacrament. And whoever believes these words has exactly what they say, 'forgiveness of sins.'"

I believe that at whatever age or stage or cognitive level we may find ourselves, we can understand and feel the real presence and the very love of God; so there is no one right time developmentally for a child to first receive holy communion. As you probably know, some of our Orthodox Christian sisters and brothers commune their infants with a small spoon on the day of their baptism, but in many traditions, a good time for First Communion is around the fifth grade. When I was in that parish in New Jersey we, too, offered First Communion instruction to fifth graders, and we held those sessions on Saturday mornings. Reflecting back on that experience, it was most often a class of sleepy-eyed, yet hyperactive children, with a few there under parental duress. We were in this together on Saturday mornings in Lent. I loved those children, always animated, stimulated, hopping around, pure energy, ready to fly, almost impossible for them to sit on a chair up to a table on Saturday morning. Yet we studied Luther's *Small Catechism*. I wondered, "Did they really understand this mystery gift of God's presence in holy communion?"

Near the end of the series, right before Easter, I asked the class, "Okay, guys, how do you really feel about holy communion? You can speak the truth." (Parents didn't attend these sessions.) "Can you think of any other experience you have had that is in any way similar to receiving holy communion?" I wasn't sure what to expect — glassy-eyed silence or adolescent sarcasm or pure heresy?

Little Chrissy, chomping on pink bubble gum, her long blond hair and skinny legs in disarray, raised her hand quickly and blurted out, wide-eyed, "Communion is like Christmas. Like Christmas when all my family gets together, and everyone's happy, and no one is yelling, and we eat a special dinner together. And we give gifts, and get gifts, and we sit around the table, and the whole family talks about what we did together last year, and we talk about and plan things to come."

Chrissy understood holy communion.

Bobby then raised his hand to speak, which was amazing in and of itself. Although always physically present, I wasn't really sure that Bobby was with us. He was an extremely quiet child who stared out the window most of the class time, in his own deep world. His parents didn't attend any church, and it was his next door neighbors who befriended him, brought him to class and worship, and were acting as his sponsors for communion. His mind and emotions, though, seemed off-limits to me. But Bobby raised his hand and looked me right in the eye and said with a certain clarity, "Holy communion is like the night right after Aunt Georgia died. People brought us tons of good food, but the whole family was so upset and crying, we didn't want to eat; until Grandma got there and said, 'Aunt Georgia is no longer in pain, she knew

Jesus and is now happy with God; you should all be happy, too, not sad, so let's eat.' "

Bobby was with us. Maybe ahead of us!

And then Harry spoke up, thinking deeply, forgetting to raise his hand. "I feel the same way about going to take communion as I felt a couple of days ago when I broke a window. I was hitting rocks with my baseball bat behind the barn, and one rock broke that dumb, small, dirty window in the storage shed."

He went on to say that he had been afraid to tell anyone about what he did, primarily out of fear of what his father would do to him. Harry Jr. ate his dinner quietly that night and, on his own, went up to bed early, but he couldn't sleep. He was restless, squirming in anguish until well after midnight, and then he couldn't stand it anymore. He was certain his father would kill him, but he had to tell his father the truth about the broken window. Trembling in fear, he got up out of bed, walked through the dark abyss of the hallway to is parents' bedroom, opened the door, entered, and walked over to his parents' bed; then he shook his father awake, and confessed.

And surprised his father squinted at him, thought for a moment, and said, "It's okay. I forgive you. Now get back to bed."

Little Harry went back to bed released from guilt and any fear. Harry said to the class that Saturday morning, "I felt great. That's the feeling I have about receiving holy communion."

Receiving gifts, sharing a meal, celebrating together, a united family, commitment, planning for the future, sensing resurrection reunion, knowing the release of forgiveness, the gift of grace, the finality of love, the real presence of God: I was being witnessed to by munchkin saints, by astute scholars of Luther and the *Catechism*, children of God ready for the holy meal — *Mandatum* Thursday

> *Just as I have loved you, so you also should love one another.* — John 13:34

> *Take and eat, take and drink, this is my body given for you; this is my blood, shed for you and for all people*

for the forgiveness of sin. Do this in remembrance of
me. — Matthew 26:29 (paraphrased)

Amen!

Sermon delivered April 9, 1998
First Lutheran Church
Duluth, Minnesota

Easter Day
Isaiah 25:6-9; Mark 16:1-8

Explaining Resurrection

Then the Lord God will wipe away the tears from all
faces. — Isaiah 25:8

Our first appointed reading from scripture this morning sets the stage for the amazing and radical confession of Easter.

When things reach completion, when time and space merge with God, when creation is fulfilled, then Isaiah 25 claims:

Then the [Lord of hosts] will destroy the shroud that is
cast over all peoples, the sheet that is spread over all
nations. [The Lord of hosts] will destroy death forever.
Then the Lord God will wipe away the tears from all
faces. — Isaiah 25:7-8 cf

According to the narrative of Saint Mark, when the sabbath was over and it was ritually, religiously legal to once again have contact with a dead body, Mary Magdalene, Mary (the mother of James), and Salome bought spices at the market stalls which were ready for business at daybreak, having been closed the whole day before. They bought spices such as myrrh to be used to properly, ritually prepare the dead body of Jesus that had been hastily buried before sundown on Friday, before the beginning of the sabbath. As the women walked to the tomb, they were experiencing the shock and grief of the recent, violent death of Jesus, and also wondering about the logistics and the emotional pain of reopening the tomb to wash and properly prepare and wrap the body.

But according to the text, when the women reached the tomb, they encountered something else — something mystifying — yet beyond shock and grief and normal assumptions.

Mark's gospel explains it this way:

> *Do not be alarmed; you are looking for Jesus of Nazareth, who was crucified. He has been raised; he is not here ... go, tell his disciples and Peter that he is going ahead of you to Galilee; there you will see him.*
> — Mark 16:6-7

There you will see him.

During final-exam week for winter term three weeks ago, we didn't have daily chapel, so I attended the weekly Bible study of some local pastors. Each Tuesday morning at eleven o'clock, they examine the Sunday morning lectionary three weeks in advance and exchange with each other thoughts about the texts and sermon suggestions. Three weeks ago, when I could attend, they considered the readings for this day — for Easter morning. The questions arose: How can one preach about "resurrection" and the living Christ? It is such a clear confession of faith — the primary confession of faith for the church. But how can you explain "Easter Resurrection" in everyday, rational language?

One pastor suggested that we say nothing; just read the gospel text, ending it with the ancient Easter greeting, "He is risen. He is risen indeed!" What more can be said? Sing the hymns and share holy communion. Easter is a confession of faith; resurrection is a glimpse into a more complete dimension of existence that is pure gift, that is the eternity of God, and basically unexplainable.

A few of the other pastors were intrigued with the messenger's curious words to the women at the tomb: "But go, tell his disciples and Peter that Jesus is going ahead of you to Galilee." And Peter! Peter who had denied Jesus three times right before Jesus was sentenced and executed. Peter who had apparently run away from an ugly situation when his friend was being tortured. The resurrected Jesus was going to Galilee for people like Peter, who is a lot like us. There was even a special invitation.

And where is this Galilee? It is where we are.

But how do you explain this as you proclaim the resurrection of Jesus to others who perhaps don't feel the same grasp of faith, and perhaps only show up at church on Easter and Christmas, out of a cultural tradition, or a spiritual longing? I believe that we must approach the event of the resurrection of Jesus head on and attempt to define and explain it, putting words to one's faith; otherwise, we may be at peace, but we will drop out of the arena of dialogue with our brothers and sisters who are seeking answers in this post-modern, science-driven world of ours.

There is today a resurgence of serious, academic interest in the historical Jesus. What did Jesus really say? What did Jesus really do? What happened? This academic quest for the historical Jesus goes back to the previous century, and the new studies have been dredging up many of the old, rationalistic explanations for the resurrection stories concerning Jesus.

Perhaps the oldest and simplest explanation for an empty tomb is the "stolen body theory." Someone, some of the disciples perhaps, stole the body from the tomb to protect it from desecration, or as some cynics contend, to purposely generate the illusion of a risen Christ. Or perhaps Joseph of Arimathea had it moved from a temporary cave-tomb near the execution site. Perhaps he moved the body very early after the sabbath for a private burial farther outside the city in his own tomb as he promised. Maybe Pontius Pilate had it moved secretly on the sabbath when the tomb area would be deserted to prevent any shrine or cult of martyrdom to develop at the grave site, which was right outside of the city gates.

The "wrong tomb" explanation theorizes: It was very early on a dim, misty morning. The women, still in despair and shock over the pain of Jesus' death and the humiliation of a Roman crucifixion, with tears in their eyes, were not really certain which of the many rock-hewn tombs in the area was the one in which Jesus was buried. When they went to the "wrong tomb," an empty tomb, they were startled by a cemetery worker who guessed their mission and tried to be helpful. "You seek Jesus of Nazareth who was crucified?" the worker asked. "He is not here." Then, pointing to the correct tomb, he said, "See the place where they laid him." The women, though, misunderstood, and ran off proclaiming resurrection.

Or there is the "lettuce theory." This is perhaps the most absurd of them all, but it is one of the oldest. Tertullian complained about the "lettuce theory" at the end of the second century AD. According to this, someone who farmed a garden plot near Joseph's tomb was so upset with curiosity seekers who came late on Friday evening, or even on the sabbath — their day off, to look at the tomb where Jesus was placed. So many came that they didn't stay on the path and inadvertently trampled the new spring crop of vegetable seedlings that had been planted near the tomb. So, late that evening, after dark, the frustrated gardener moved the body to another location, hoping the crowds would go away.

Or the "swoon theory." Jesus "almost" died on the cross. "Almost!" There were no machines to monitor brain waves. After his rapid burial before the fast approaching sabbath, the coolness of the tomb helped to revive Jesus. The grave wrappings stopped fatal bleeding.

There are other such theories, many from the nineteenth century, some quite early: the "hallucination theory," the "twin brother theory," and the "rapid-decay hypothesis."

Many of these explanations carry the weight of religious prejudice, some a bit of desperation, while others are more serious attempts to rationally explain away something that seems beyond possibility or objective probability.

Well, what happened? It was certainly an "event" in history, in the sense that something happened that caused a dramatic change in the mood and outlook of the disciples and other previous followers of Jesus. People went from utter despair expecting nothing following the cruel death of a crucifixion, from expecting nothing more, to proclaiming personal encounters with a living Christ. It happened in many different places to a variety of people.

One aspect of the story that helps to convince me about the reality of the Easter resurrection is that it was perceived not as a rumor of something that happened but as a personal experience that was later defined in many different but personalized ways. As a related example, I observed something once that I have not told many people about, and yet it has left a lasting image in my mind.

When I was about ten or eleven years old, my father was an elected delegate to the national convention of our Lutheran church. He went by car with the New Jersey Synod delegation to the convention held that year in Iowa. In my satisfied, parochial view of the world at that time, I envisioned Iowa as "out there" somewhere on the western fringe of existence with other exotic western states such as North Dakota and Ohio. My brothers and Mom and I all missed him that week Dad was away.

But on the day of his return, a Saturday, my brothers and I, anxiously waiting, were playing in the living room, occasionally getting up to look out the window to see if the car we heard passing by would stop and release our father. We waited most of the afternoon.

And then, joyous time, the car in which he and the other delegates from the shore had traveled west, pulled up in front of our house. There was Dad getting his suitcase out of the trunk. My brothers ran out the door and I went to get Mom. She was in the bedroom, the door was closed, the window curtains drawn, the lights out. I yelled, "Dad's home!" and knocked on the door. It opened slightly. Mom said in a halting, haunting voice that I still remember, "Do you see him? Do you see him?"

I said, "Yes, come on!"

She came to the door with hollow, red eyes — the eyes of one in sorrow. It startled me a bit. As I headed to the front door, she went to the front window first to see for herself, and then she ran outside and jumped into my father's arms, almost knocking over my little brothers. We were all glad to see Dad, but I thought Mom was *really* glad to see him.

Well, Dad had some trip presents from the western frontier for us children, and while we were fooling around with the gifts, I overheard some private, adult conversation. Apparently, earlier in the day some parishioner had called my mother and said she had heard on the radio that a Robert Wuchter was killed in an automobile accident, and she wanted to offer us condolences and share our grief.

So Mom asked from the darkness of the room of her soul, in shock, alarmed, desperate, "Do you see him?" But our word was not enough, even in light of her hope. She had to leap into his arms and know for sure it was he.

Jesus really died. Roman executioners knew death, even to ramming a spear into the corpse. Serious historians do not debate the completed murder of Jesus. But in Galilee and beyond, something happened beyond rumor and in the realm of pure personal experience — more than hearing or just seeing but being profoundly, existentially touched by the living Christ. It is faith that involves body, mind, and soul, though the resurrected Jesus was not the same as before; all the various resurrection accounts agree on that. There was a transformation, though personhood was in place. I believe it is a foretaste of our own possible future with God.

Whatever resurrection is, according to the Christian confession, from the moment of Easter on, nothing can be the same for the end or completion of creation has been previewed in the death and resurrection of Jesus on the cross. All safety and wholeness is somehow in the love that was lived by Jesus — a love expressed in such acts as liberation, healing, forgiveness, compassion, sacrifice, and peace-making — this love manifest in Jesus and even available through us as we serve others in Christlike actions is what the harmony and final balance of creation is all about, including our eternal future.

> *Do not be alarmed; you are looking for Jesus of Nazareth, who was crucified. He has been raised and he is going ahead of you to Galilee; and there you will see him, experience him, which is to experience God — available, present in Galilee or wherever you happen to be.* — Mark 16:6-7 (paraphrased)

He is risen! He is risen indeed! Amen.

Sermon delivered April 3, 1994
Weaver Chapel
Wittenberg University
Springfield, Ohio

Christ In Guatemala

They were startled and terrified, and thought that they
were seeing a ghost. — Luke 24:37

While the disciples were still talking about Christ's appearance at Emmaus, Jesus himself stood among them and said to them,

"Peace be with you." They were startled and fright-
ened, thinking they saw a ghost. He said, "Why are you
troubled, and why do doubts rise in your minds? It is
myself! Touch me. A ghost does not have flesh and
bones." — Luke 24:36-39 (paraphrased)

Imagine this, for it, too, has some flesh and bones ... You are passenger on the *Southern Chief*, an Amtrak train that runs the Texas to southern California route. The train is hitting seventy miles an hour about fifteen miles southeast of Santa Fe, New Mexico, and is entering a long ravine about 2:30 in the afternoon. The sky is overcast, yet a bright white. The scenery is stark, but striking. It is desert. It is cacti and sage brush and delicate violet asters and red rock cliffs all passing by your window; and then all of a sudden you see — what? — apparitions in the desert? Apparitions, and they are dancing — wild dancers dressed in flowing clothes of bright blue turquoise and pink and spring green. They are hooded dancers, spinning wildly, streamers and feathers attached to their heads. Some of the figures are tall, some are small, some dance on top of a cliff, some dance down near the tracks in the ravine; all are spinning and dancing. What is this — a desert dreamscape?

One of the apparitions seems to wave; and then they are gone as the train hurdles west, up out of the ravine, around a bend, more desert and red rock and sagebrush but no apparitions, no dancers. Were they ghosts? What is this? Is it a mid-afternoon dream conjuring up the spirits of long dead Anasazi or Inca Indians or an optical illusion? Others on the train have seen them, too. People are amazed. "What was that we saw together?" You wonder, and people talk to others on the train, with strangers who become no longer strangers. There are a lot of theories, and everyone looks more intently out the train window at the desert from now on, laughing together; and they remember. Things have changed. Really changed.

While the disciples were still talking about Christ's apparent appearance at Emmaus, Jesus himself stood among them and said to them,

> *"Peace be with you!" They were startled and terrified and thought that they were seeing a ghost. He said to them, "Why are you frightened, and why do doubts arise in your hearts? Look at my hands and my feet; see that it is I myself. Touch me and see; for a ghost does not have flesh and bones, as you see that I have."*
> — Luke 24:36b-39

Not a dream as pure illusion, but rather grounded in some expression of reality — something real that one can touch.

Fifteen miles southeast of Santa Fe in the desert ravine near Canyoncito, New Mexico, the apparitions' names were Victoria and Sherie and Dianne and Dianne's nine-year-old daughter, Bridey, and there is also Ifan with Sandino, the dog. They had worn hooded costumes made by Vickie of long flowing cloth, some of it made from bright-colored curtains and an old flag, all covered with beads and bells and buttons. Who are these people?

They are dream dancers, part of a project called "Apparitions and Amtrak," funded in part by a grant from the National Endowment for the Arts and the New Mexico State Division of Arts.

"We are reminders to the train passengers," said Vicki from behind her long, flowing, green-velvet mask that is sewn to a wrangler's hat. "We are reminders to the train passengers that dreams are important aspects of our lives."

But more than just dreams alone, they are dreams that are formed by real flesh and bone people. You could touch them if the train would have stopped and they let you touch them. They are real but they also did really generate images of dreams and thoughts and wonder, and strangers were transformed into friends, and history came alive, and the desert didn't seem so stark any longer. Some new things happened for real, though the train passengers certainly didn't and don't know all the details about these dancers in the desert, but they were not ghosts.

When I was in Guatemala City before Holy Week this year, there was a strange occurrence one evening. My group had eaten a late dinner in a restaurant in the old center section of the city a mile or two from our hotel. After dinner, I decided to wander around the town. There is not a lot of traffic in Guatemala City, but on one main street downtown, suddenly, traffic was backed up, cars were stopped, and drivers were honking car horns. Everyone was trying to find some side streets to take to get out of the tie up.

Then up ahead, beyond where the traffic was stopped, in the middle of the street, I noticed a lighted object moving and swaying and coming toward me. As I walked closer, it also came closer to me, and then I could see what it was coming down the street. It was Jesus! It was a giant Jesus — Jesus nailed to a cross.

There was a big, red, lighted sign hanging out in front of a store that said, "Levi's," and Jesus had to be careful not to bang into it. There was a Pizza Hut, believe it or not, in downtown Guatemala City, right on a street corner where there was also a charcoal fire over which barefooted Mayan Indians were roasting corn. Gliding by both the Pizza Hut and the Indians on the street was Jesus on the cross, blood running down his face from a crown of thorns, and dripping from hand and feet. The spear had already been thrust in his side. It was a twenty-foot Jesus nailed to a cross and raised on a platform that was carried through the streets by at least thirty men. A portable generator trailed behind the float so that Jesus could be lit even brighter than the Pizza Hut sign and the red Levi's sign, certainly brighter than the charcoal fire of the street-corner Indians who made the sign of the cross as their crucified Savior passed by.

Straw had been placed along the path of the procession, and the lighted Jesus came down the main street to the gate of the cathedral, where it entered the courtyard, was turned all around by the thirty men, and then Jesus entered the tall, wide-open doors of the cathedral to the sound of a brass band. I was surrounded by hundreds of people. Some pious believers were in town and on the square that night to see this Lenten procession; and others were downtown for a movie or for some action but were surprised by the presence of Jesus. Now together, planned and spontaneous, we all watched Jesus, nailed to a cross, come down the main street of the city, and we all followed Jesus into the church.

But more was happening here than just a parade. Marching in front of the statue was a line of hooded college students who represented death. Covered with hoods they represented all those who bring death, and especially, they represented the ones who had crucified Jesus — those who had nailed him to the cross.

In Guatemala City there is also in the center of town less than a block from this church cathedral, a massive fortress-like building that is the main office of the national police force. The national police force has been accused of forming the death squads that have killed thousands of peasants and Indians in the night — church leaders and political organizers — throughout the last decade. Those in the procession who represented the murderers of Christ stopped in front of the police station and started calling out and chanting for the police to join them as the killers of Christ.

The police did charge out with guns drawn and clubs raised, people screamed and ran back toward the church, and in the midst of all this, it became very apparent that this was more than just lifeless symbolism — Christ *was* there, for real! Here, too, were those who feared a loss of human power and who raised their guns and clubs to crucify him again. You could have gone out into the street and felt the touch of the clubs; they were very real, as real as the nails for the cross, and as real as the blood that flowed that night from some of the students who were beaten. You could see that these people were not ghosts. It was very real — the gospel story of the road to Golgotha was spoken again; it lived again.

Touch all of this if you dare.

*They were startled and frightened, thinking at first that
perhaps they had seen a ghost. He said. "Why do doubts
rise in your minds? It is myself! Touch me. A ghost does
not have flesh and bones that can be broken."*
— Luke 24:36-39 (paraphrased)

One of my doctoral advisors from Princeton Seminary wrote in a recently published book, "Some of the most beautiful music I ever heard was the chanting of Greek peasant women, tears streaming down their lined and hardened faces, in a church on Corfu one Good Friday evening. I asked someone, 'Why are they weeping?' "

"Because," I was told, "their Christ is dead."

"I have often thought," he wrote, "that I will never understand what resurrection means until I can weep like that."

I bet if he had gone back on Easter, their pure joy would have been just as authentic and deeply felt. The resurrected Christ is just as real.

What is it that forms our perception of reality?

One of William Blake's more famous passages describes his reaction to a sunrise, as opposed to what people see. Blake wrote, "Why, it will be questioned, when the sun rises, do you not see a round disc of fire somewhat like a gold coin? [Just a ball of burning gas this morning sun?] Oh no! No, I see an innumerable company of the heavenly host crying, 'Holy, Holy, Holy is the Lord God Almighty.' " Not ghosts — not an illusion — but the reality of creation praising the Creator.

The Easter ending to the biblical story holds much confusion in regard to the details. Each of the gospel authors tells the details of the story differently; resurrection was and is experienced differently as to the details, but what they all firmly agreed upon in the biblical record was that something happened that split the darkness of life. Look to the end of the story for the good news. At first, the women were running away from the tomb trembling bewildered and too fearful to tell anyone what they had discovered at the tomb. In today's reading from Luke, there was fear and trembling in the upper room, the disciples startled and frightened, thinking they had seen a ghost. The problem at this level was that they were still looking for Christ among the dead, and we do the same only as history. A dead Jesus offends no one. A dead Jesus can make people sad or uneasy or even frightened, but the resurrection seen as an event that was and is real makes all the difference in regard to grounding our hope in God's reality and challenging us to become Christlike.

A resurrection revealing a living Christ puts us directly into the story. The good news is that Christ is not in the tomb, in the past, but is now and also future, going on before us to Galilee, sharing food and good news with us on the way to Emmaus. Christ is entering in the midst of our gathering, seen in others in the trains and planes we travel, coming down our main streets, crucified again in each injustice, or lifting us up in real forgiveness and healing. Something very real is acting through the compassionate actions of a stranger or perhaps using our real flesh and blood and mind to forge divine love into freedom or justice. And it is real! You can touch it; it can touch you.

> *While they were talking about Christ, Christ stood among them and said to them, "Peace be with you." At first they were startled and frightened, thinking they saw a ghost. Christ said to them, "Why are you troubled, and why do doubts rise in your minds? ... Touch me and see; a ghost does not have flesh and bones, as you see I have."* — Luke 24:36-39 (paraphrased)

Sermon delivered April 17, 1988
Weaver Chapel
Wittenberg University
Springfield, Ohio

Missions

*But in your hearts sanctify Christ as Lord. Always be
ready to make your defense to any one who demands
from you an accounting for the hope that is in you.*
— 1 Peter 3:15

*I will not leave you desolate; I will come to you ... be-
cause I live, you will live also ... he who loves me will
be loved by my Father, and I will love him and manifest
myself to him.*   — John 14:18-21 (RSV)

The above verses offer advice and support for our mission as
Christians.

A lot of diverse people, groups, and agencies are talking about
"their mission" today, about their purpose and goals — government agencies, school boards, candidates for public office. My old
college recently set up a "Commission on Mission and Priorities."

It turned out a 36-page report, summarized as follows: "Our
University's fundamental purpose — mission — is to help educate
the creative minority of a civilization, to develop in harmony the
intellectual, spiritual, social, and physical qualities which charac-
terize wholeness of person." A mission statement. Pretty general,
but maybe that's where we have to start. What's our mission, as
Christians, today?

On last week's vacation, I had time to wander through some
museums. One of the current displays at the Museum of Modern
Art in New York was a number of examples of Mexican Art and
illustrations from the early 1900s up into the 1930s. The mission
of those artists was to express the depression of the times — the

poverty — the political corruption — the cheapness of life during revolution — the fear of Fascism.

Their artwork was in dull and dark colors picturing symbols of death and dust. There were grim reapers riding on starved horses, insect-like leaders, shattered promises — all this displayed in small windowless rooms. After a while, I just wanted to get out of that show, and get outside into the sunshine and fresh air. The artists accomplished their mission quite effectively. They portrayed their interpretation of life at that time and place.

What interpretation of life and future do we wish to portray or make real to those around us as part of our Christian mission?

An artist with a different mission was portrayed at the Metropolitan Museum of Art. The name of the show was "Monet's Years at Giverny: Beyond Impressionism." The exhibit was composed of 81 paintings by Claude Monet that were painted in his later years at his estate in the town of Giverny, France, about forty miles north of Paris on a branch of the river Seine.

Monet planted flowers everywhere on the few acres of his estate — flowerbed after flowerbed, plus flowering trees, rose bushes, wisteria on the foot bridge, and of course, water lilies in the pond. His home was a blaze of color from early spring until late fall. Monet's paintings captured this splash of color and order and life.

Monet wrote that his mission was to share his sense of joy and color, creativity and change that he sensed all around him. When he gave his large water lily series to the government of France, which built a special circular room in a museum to display them. Monet wrote that he wanted these paintings to bring joy and calmness into the life of the one viewing the paintings — a place where people pushed around by the pressures of daily work and living could come to calm down, relax, put things back into perspective.

And Monet completed his mission — his paintings do just what he wanted.

What is your mission, as other people view your life as a living picture? What are your priorities, your hope for others?

For the last few weeks, our first lesson reading has been from the book of the Acts of the Apostles — the acts of the first, second, and third generation of Christians — as they attempted to define their mission.

Probably the most impressive aspect of their outlook on life was their feeling that they were being led in their mission — they weren't on their own in the struggle. They felt that the "Spirit of God's truth" was with them, and it gave to these early Christians a devastating freedom.

They were not always asking, "What will work? What will be the strategy of our success?" The single existential question of their lives was, "What does God will us to do next?"

They were not slaves to their own ambitions. Realistic strategies of action are necessary, but a sense of God's presence and purpose is of primary importance. One's success or failure is not dependent on strategies that work or do not work.

It's like the father who bought a backyard swing set for his children. He went out in the backyard and dumped out all the pipes and parts in a pile, and his children and all their neighborhood friends formed an anxious circle around him. He started fitting and screwing and bracing the set together. As it began to near completion — and the children were getting restless — he realized that the last few parts just did not fit together, and there were pieces missing. In disgust, as the children rode off on their bicycles, he started pulling the pieces apart and putting them back in the box for the trip back to Kiddy City or Builder's Emporium. At that moment, out of the box fell the little book of directions. On the cover was printed something like, "When all else fails, follow these instructions." The set did fit together, and all the pieces were there.

Early Christians claimed that God doesn't really offer specific detailed directions (some code of ethics) for each of our actions, but does promise that in him the pieces do ultimately fit together. There is a purpose, a center to one's existence. Our mission, first, is to sense this will and freedom, to sense the "Spirit of truth," active around us, in others, available.

Our gospel author tries hard to define our mission. "We love, because he first loved us." Mission is coming home — back to the center of things.

Jesus is speaking to people who have experienced his love and care for them. The love they sense in him and feel for him is precisely the love they are to feel for God, and the translation of this love into action is to flow out of their sense of their won value as loved persons, and be expressed toward those around them.

They don't have to do this on the basis of a fading memory of this person of Jesus who loved in the past, because this Christ lives now. We are not godforsaken.

The Spirit of truth: God is here, creating now, through us, calling people home. It forms our mission.

This may be threatening to people who see God as removed from the daily action of life, or God as an oriental tyrant type or ruthless judge or a joke or a nonentity or see purpose based in fame or power or an efficient police force keeping order by use of our animal fear of death or punishment.

We have a difficult mission to define love to people in a transient, fragmented society where relationships often tend to be so brief and fragile and irresponsible. We have a mission of love to those around us who are frantically attempting to hide deep fears of worthlessness who, with perhaps a cocky attitude, are trying to compensate for the suspicion that they have no value at all.

We have a mission to communicate the gospel, the goodness of God's lasting love, to people in ways that penetrate the armor of their despair. Strength for mission is a valid way of spreading the good news by supporting the work of people who share our purpose.

Behind this important strategy has to be our individual understanding of mission. Every congregation must have a missionary structure, each person actually, with a sense of a missionary responsibility for one's own neighborhood. Mission is a calling home.

In John 13, Jesus told his closest friends,

> *A new commandment I give you: love one another. As I have loved you, so you must love one another. If you have love for one another, then all will know that you are my disciples.* — John 13:34-35 (paraphrased)

That's a mission — a calling — a purpose — a direction.

Our mission is a commitment to pray and act, to give evidence of our devotion to the God who "so loved the world that he gave his only Son."

We need a renewed focus on our call as the baptized children of God to speak about and give evidence of what we have seen, heard, and experienced in God's love for the world.

Our mission is to allow the Holy Spirit to work through us, to pray that the Spirit will give us renewed confidence to speak his name to our world. Our mission is to act for others, to serve with compassion, to call for justice for his children, to call people home, to the center of things.

Our mission of stewardship therefore requires that we love not only our own, but those who are strange and alien to us.

We need to open our community of faith — to share that faith with others.

We pray for strength to enable more effective service, and for new confidence to speak to and for others in his name.

Asking for strength for mission is a prayer for a new and re-newed beginning, for a return to our origins as beings created by God in his image; we pray for that kind of strength, and creativity, to make our mission alive for others. In Christ's name we pray. Amen.

Sermon delivered April 30, 1978
Resurrection Lutheran Church
Hamilton Square, New Jersey

Friendship

*As the Father has loved me, so I have loved you; abide
in my love. If you keep my commandments, you will
abide in my love, just as I have kept my Father's commandments and abide in his love. I have said these
things to you so that my joy may be in you, and that
your joy may be complete.*

*This is my commandment, that you love one an-
other as I have loved you. No one has greater love than
this, to lay down one's life for one's friends. You are my
friends if you do what I command you. I do not call you
servants any longer, because the servant does not know
what the master is doing; but I have called you friends,
because I have made known to you everything that I
have heard from my Father. You did not choose me but
I chose you. And I appointed you to go and bear fruit,
fruit that will last, so that the Father will give you whatever you ask him in my name. I am giving you these
commands so that you may love one another.*

— John 15:9-17

The gospel of the Lord!

This "gospel text" is alive with possibilities for reflection. I
consider it a pretty bold and courageous statement. It attempts to
uncover the very essence of God by carefully offering what was at
the time a new definition of "love." The text states that the life of
Jesus defines this love. The confession here is that Jesus' life is a
pure expression of God. The way Jesus "loved" people is a sharp
picture of what God is. That's the confession this morning, and a
command! "This is my commandment, that you love one another
as I have loved you." The people that Jesus loved had the same

basic needs, fears, and concerns that we all have, and that all our neighbors have.

This text also attempts to define the source of human joy; what makes us complete and therefore "at peace" and joyful. A joy even in the midst of this sacrificial love that Jesus lived. "No one has greater love than this, to lay down one's life for one's friends," said Jesus. And yet even here, he claimed, is joy!

There is one key concept interwoven in all of this that I have not specifically addressed in past sermons on this text. It is a definition of "friend." According to the book of John, Jesus said, "You are my friends if you do what I ask. (If you follow me and enact my love.) I do not call you servants any longer, because the servant does not know the master's plan. But I have called you friends, because I have made known to you everything that I have learned from my Father." "Everything that I feel and know about God, I have shared with you, and therefore in this mutual confession we can now be true friends to one another."

"Friends." We have to be careful here because our culture uses that word in a variety of discordant ways just like it uses and defines in multiple ways the word "love." But what did the very early church mean by "friend"? What did Jesus mean when he said to his followers, "I now call you friends"?

There are some common assumptions about the nature of friendship that I used to think were compatible with my faith but in the light of today's text, I no longer think they are compatible. I have often said to people in the past that "a person is very lucky if he or she has even two or three friends in their whole lifetime. Friends are such a rare and blessed gift." But according to Jesus, we are called into a community of friendship, a vast community of friends. As Christians we are all called to be more than servants of one another but also friends. My old opinion that we would be very lucky to have only two or three kindred spirits in our lifetime is based on the desire to find someone who is just like us, someone who thinks the same, has the same likes and dislikes, and the same tastes. It all goes beyond sharing core values. Such a kindred spirit certainly could be a blessing, but Jesus, I believe, expects more from us.

Another "friendship myth" that I have come to question is one I learned in seminary and heard restated just two weeks ago at a regional gathering of Lutheran pastors. We had a guest presenter, and we were talking together about the responsibilities and pressures of being Lutheran clergy in post-modern times. The presenter brought up from the reservoir of old conventional wisdom that pastors shouldn't really make friends with anyone in their congregation. This is just asking for all kinds of trouble. This standard advice usually comes with a list of reasons and horror stories to back it up: Such relationships will cause resentment among parishioners who are not in the circle of friendship with the pastor. It will cloud the pastor's prophetic voice if a word of judgment should be spoken to those who are friends. If you are supposed to openly share the trials and tribulations of your life with true friends, should you really share the things that are bugging you about the congregation with people who are also members of that congregation? If you are having some personal problems or worries or doubts and you share that with friends who are parishioners, won't they begin to question your qualifications to fulfill the role of pastor? There is a whole well-worn list of reasons given why pastors should not make friends with parishioners.

I told my colleagues that I thought that this conventional wisdom was wrong. There are always certain boundaries that must be kept; there are things concerning individuals and the job that I don't share with anyone, including my wife. There are professional responsibilities in regard to confidentiality, as there are in other professions. There are some realities about people's perceptions, whether they are good or bad, which must be respected. But for the most part, I believe that old conventional wisdom about a pastor never making friends within the congregation is very wrong. I believe this advice is based on some past models for ministry that are not appropriate for the church that believes all members must be a team sharing a mutual call to ministry in this present age. We are called to be friends. This was certainly the way the church envisioned itself at its birth when Jesus said to his followers, "You are my friends, and you are to be friends to one another."

Well, all the pastors at this meeting disagreed with me, which often seems to happen when I get together with pastors to discuss priorities or strategies for ministry. I am afraid some priorities are inadvertently defending old models of ministry based on control and hierarchy, and interfering with our mutual call to engage those outside of the faith with God's living word. Plus, Jesus called us all to be friends.

I think we should re-examine our understanding of "friendship" in light of our gospel text this morning — the voice of the earliest church. What did Jesus mean when he called us to be friends?

It is something very different from what our surrounding culture sometimes calls "friendship" where the goal is to be acquainted with people more popular than oneself — people of assumed power and prestige so that hopefully you can by association gain these properties from the other for your self. It is that desire to be "seen with the right people." Here, friendships are dropped quickly or just ignored if circumstances change. One of the most painful experiences we can have is discovering that people we thought valued us — valued our friendship — didn't really value us at all.

I read an autobiographical reflection by a rather well-known person who shared one of his most painful experiences. As a child he was very quiet and shy, and not very athletically inclined, so he was not sought after in team sports. He was basically ignored by his classmates and neighborhood children, until his parents installed a swimming pool in the backyard. (You know what is coming!) All of a sudden he was popular with lots of newfound friends. But when other pools, many larger and more ornately landscaped, were later installed at other homes, this boy's backyard was no longer the gathering place. He remembers actually saying to his mother on a hot and lonely summer day, "Mom, the kids really didn't care about me at all, did they? They cared about the pool." He wrote, "That is one of the most painful experiences we ever face in a relationship — the experience of discovering people we thought valued us and valued the relationship didn't really value us or the relationship at all. They valued us only because of what they thought the relationship gave them access to." It's "being used"! The story could be replayed substituting the job, sex, or wealth for the pool. All is separated totally from any profound desire just for the well-being of the other. The desire for the wholeness of the other, the wellness of the other, this is the "friendship" that Jesus calls us into.

I want to give credit to the book, *Bread for the Journey*, by Henri Nouwen. Many of my following thoughts and some of my words have been influenced by this devotional book, which I believe is excellent. To be honest with you, I have tried many daily, devotional booklets through the years, and I rarely found one that I even liked a little bit. I would start most of them and never finish them. I would rather do my own diverse reading and listening and then form my own devotional thoughts and prayerful petitions. But I have found this book very different. *Bread for the Journey*'s two or so paragraphs for each day are consistently deep and revealing. And throughout this devotional, Nouwen has woven the concept of "friendship" in a way that I believe matches the command of Jesus in today's gospel text.

What is this "friendship" into which all Christians have been called? "A friend lays down her life for the other," said Jesus. A friend makes his own life — his own sorrow and joy, own despair and hope, own loneliness and experience of intimacy — available to others as a source of life for the other. One of the greatest gifts we can give others is ourselves, especially in their times of crisis. It is when we proclaim by our presence, "Do not be afraid. I want to know what you are living, and I will attempt to live it with you. You are not alone. I am here." The friend plays the role of God. It is this friendship that destroys loneliness. One is not lonely in the presence of a friend.

Friendship is in the caring presence of another even if no words are spoken. Sharing our solitude, our silence, our inner prayer; we can be still with a friend and both know that God is there with us.

Sometimes, in life, our sorrow overwhelms us so much that we no longer can even believe in joy. In those times we need our friends to hold our hand and assist us to start taking steps again in the direction of peace, in the direction of joy. Even when we are not yet able to feel the truth of what they say, being there we can begin to feel the joy that seemed to be lost, and our life can become livable again.

Friends have no need to pretend. Friendship is when the gamesmanship of daily life is over. No demands need be made. God's love is unconditional. Friends can share ill-conceived thoughts, fears, and doubts without the fear of being belittled or made fun of.

Friends are free gifts from God. Friends cannot be made, but God gives us the friends we need when we need them if we fully trust in God's love. Friends cannot replace God. Friends always have limitations and weaknesses like we all have. Their love is never faultless, never complete; but in their limitations they can be guideposts on our journey toward the unlimited and unconditional love of God.

Friends are good listeners with no inner needs to make their own presence known — just free to receive, to welcome, to accept. Listening is a form of spiritual hospitality by which one invites even strangers to become friends. There is a warning here for congregations. Congregations should always remember that true friendship creates space where strangers can enter and become friends. Whenever a strong sense of community is present, and we easily can talk about our congregation as a "family," there is also the temptation to slip into elitism and exclusivism, which makes outsiders of everyone else. Biblical friendship is an ongoing expression of hospitality always wishing to welcome all outsiders into the family of friendship. Jesus calls us to love even our enemies. Our call is to bring all others into the circle of friendship.

Friendship is a bond beyond common goals, common interests, or common histories, because it is based on a bond deeper than even a shared fate can solidify. It is a unity of souls that gives nobility and sincerity to the fact that the love of God will *never* abandon us.

No two friends are the same. Each has his or her own gift for us. When we expect one friend to have everything we need, we will always be disappointed. One friend may offer us affection, another may stimulate our minds, another may strengthen our souls. The more able we are to receive the different gifts that our friends have to offer, the more able we will be to offer our own unique but also limited gifts. It means always treating the other as an equal, realizing that different gifts of ability, intelligence, talents, or insight can all speak to the beauty of God's creation.

Henri Nouwen stated in *Bread for the Journey* that there is a "twilight zone" in our own hearts that we ourselves cannot see. Even when we know quite a bit about ourselves — our gifts and weaknesses, our ambitions and aspirations, our motives and drives. Large parts of who we are remain in the shadow of our consciousness. We are always partially hidden to ourselves. But friends can often see into our twilight zones better than we can ourselves; and we will never fully know our own significance in the lives of our friends. This is a grace-gift that calls us not only into humility but also into a deep trust in those who love us and can make us known to ourselves.

Also woven into the command of Jesus to be friends is the call to be friends to ourselves. Do we love who we are? It is difficult to develop friendships with others until we have befriended ourselves. If we can trust that we are embraced and loved by God, we can befriend ourselves and then reach out to others in loving relationships. "Love your neighbor as you love yourself."

Friendship, as it was lived by Jesus, is the model for us. Friendship heals, brings union and equality, respects and knows the sacred nature of the other, and allows us to see our own sacred purpose. Friendship is a relationship where resurrection dominates. Friendship is to be for another, and to act for the other, even at a cost to oneself. It is living for the *other* person and finding *yourself* in the process.

I am going to let Saint John summarize and give the final word:

> *As the Father has loved me, so I have loved you; [said Jesus] abide in my love. I have said these things to you so that my joy may be in you, and that your joy may be complete. Love one another as I have loved you. You are my friends when you follow my example. I have*

called you friends, because I have made known to you
everything that I have heard from my Father.
— John 15:9-15 (paraphrased)

Amen.

Sermon delivered May 28, 2000
First Lutheran Church
Duluth, Minnesota

Parenting And Hiking

*I am the good shepherd [said Jesus]. The good shep-
herd lays down his life for the sheep.* — John 10:11

A shepherd. Do you know any shepherds? I have a cousin who
was once a shepherd. I think it was part of her hippie phase, back
in the late '60s or early '70s. She lived for a short time on a farm in
New England as an artist, but part of her day was spent caring for a
small herd of sheep and goats. Their wool was used for weaving,
and cheese was made from the goats' milk. She learned that being
a shepherd was not easy work. She also learned that each of the
sheep and goats had a unique personality. They were like little children. Sometimes the sheep would do things to endanger themselves
like getting stuck in fences or eating the wrong weeds in the field
and getting sick. Sometimes, the goats would long for freedom
higher up on the mountain, and they would escape into the forest,
although they probably would not have lasted long on their own.

At the time and place of Jesus, everyone knew shepherds. They
were a part of the tribe, a part of the family. Everyone was pretty
much aware of the trials and tribulations of being a shepherd, along
with the great responsibility. Sheep and goats were very valuable,
often the very existence of the clan or village was dependent on the
well-being of the sheep and goats.

The term "shepherd" also held a lot of symbolic importance
at the time of Jesus. The Jewish religion and the religions of surrounding cultures used "shepherd" as a metaphor to describe a
God who cared for the individual, and who would take risks to
rescue the lost or wandering individual even though the sheep, for
the most part, are oblivious to these grace gifts from the "good

shepherd"; oblivious to the fact that they were dependent on God for life itself.

Both these contact points are pretty much lost in our time and culture. Few of us know a shepherd or the trials and tribulations of that occupation; and if we are going to witness to those on the edge of faith about the reality and nature of God, I think we should use a more recognizable symbol today than that of a shepherd.

I believe that if Jesus restated this gospel reading claim and challenge for us he would say something like, "I am the good mother." "I am the loving parent who lays down her life for the child." Today's text is just perfect for "Mothers' Day"!

In the novel, *The Good Mother*, by Sue Miller, during a meal Anna cannot take her eyes off her young daughter. Anna reflects, "I never tired of looking at her. Sometimes she'd find it annoying, as though I were taking something from her by loving her so greedily with my eyes, 'Don't look at me, Mommy,' she'd say, and cover her eyes with her hands as though then I couldn't see her anymore."

Anna ran the water into the tub to bathe her toddler after spending time together in the sun and at play. And the mother, again, closely watched her child. "Her body seemed insubstantial, gleamed white as a dream as she jumped around naked. [But] when I switched on the yellowing light in the bathroom ... her skin was rough and gray on her knees and sunburned pink on her shoulders — I was startled by her solidity ... I wanted to freeze the moment, to make myself remember everything about it. It seemed one of those momentary revelations of the harmony and beauty that underlie domestic life, a gift."[1]

This novel did not just portray an idealized image of mothering. According to the story line, this mother knew well the struggles along with the joys of contemporary family life from the pull between career and mothering, to our cultural atmosphere of stranded and broken marriages, to the tension that builds when there are serious differences of opinion, or goals and hopes, in child raising. Then there are the crushing responsibilities, the never-ending decision making. But in the splashing waters of the bath that day, Anna sensed a greater intention for goodness and harmony housed in the glistening personhood of her daughter, and the "good mother" wanted only the best that love could offer for this other life. That's what is "good" here. That's the "good shepherd" in all of this! She wanted only the best that only love could offer for the other — the other sacred life.

We are not God, nor is our life now in total union with God. Mothers' Day can also remind us of the flaws of our human journey. Like when death intervenes. Some of us have lost a mother to death recently. For some of us parents, it was a child who died. Some of our mothers are captured by Alzheimer's disease at this moment. Some of us can only wish we could have a child. Some of our parents were not as nurturing or kind as they should have been, or could have been. But Good Shepherd Sunday, and Mother's Day, is the time to celebrate and reflect on the "good mother" — those moments when a parent reflects the very nature of God; those moments of deep desire for only the best that love can offer another life. It enriches all of us!

For those of us who have raised children, or have closely watched child raising in our extended family, or in remembering our own journey into maturity in the shadow of our own parents or adult guides — you know the wonderful and treacherous journey child raising represents. But what a grand adventure!

Our two children are now out of the home, and the journey of concern and love for them never ends, but the first chapters of the story have been completed for us. Although the impact of the events in those chapters continue. But, our intense day-to-day time together as parents with children is now completed. I thought of this as Shirley and I were hiking just two weeks ago, when we completed the Superior Hiking Trail. We knew we were nearing the end of that goal. We had previously walked about 200 miles of the trail and had less than thirty miles to go, so two weeks ago, we left right after the 10:45 service on Sunday and got in a good section of trail before dark. We stayed over in Grand Marais and then polished off the remaining miles. It was a wonderful journey, hiking this trail over the last couple of years. We actually walked it twice because most often we would park, walk six miles in or so, mark the map, and turn around and walk back to the car.

This personal commitment to walk the whole trail was a lot like parenting. It was a grand adventure with a lot of mystery. When we started we weren't sure what we were getting into. And like the parenting of young children, it all went by much too fast. In the beginning, as we looked at those 230 or so miles of trail on the map, it seemed like a timeless and endless task, a challenging and positive long-term commitment, and then it was over. It seemed like the children who grow up so fast — too fast.

We tried to do the project right. We took no shortcuts, and rather fanatically checked out each campsite. We walked all the spur trails and examined all the scenic overlooks. We read Brazelton and all the latest studies on child care and child development. We didn't want to shortchange our children or miss anything, or do it wrong, this parenting.

A good motto for hiking and child raising is "expect the unexpected." And the unexpected is not always fun. One section on the trail not too far outside of Two Harbors, looks on the map just like any other mile through the forest. But this section of the trail also serves in the winter as a snowmobile trail. To accommodate the machines, the trail must be wider than the normal hiking path, which changes the integrity of the forest. Drainage is altered and the path becomes often soupy and muddy in the spring and early summer. With no tree canopy, the sunlight reaches the ground and nourishes tall grass. The day I walked this section, the grass on the trail was a bright, new green, wet from an early morning rain, and up above my knee level.

I don't know if this is the proper terminology to use here, but in fly-fishing one talks about a "hatch." When the temperature and moisture are just right for the birth of a particular species of fly or other insect, there is a hatch; a birth-burst of life and that type of fly is everywhere along the stream. Well, this day on that grassy mile-long stretch of trail there had been a "hatch," a birth-burst of ticks. There were hundreds and hundreds of wood ticks; actually, along that mile of trail there were thousands of ticks. It was a wet, humid, hot day, and I was hiking in shorts.

Normally I find insects interesting, but the thought of something boring under my skin made me anxious and uncomfortable.

It altered my hiking schedule and my expectations, having to stop every fifty yards or so to pick off the ticks before they went down my socks, or up my pants. Not very pleasant. But I was soon back in the forest again and the tick encounter could then be placed into proper perspective. It became a chapter in the story of the trail that I can now laugh at.

Child raising has a lot of those experiences: unexpected moments when routine joy is broken by an unexpected, unpleasant occurrence, a sickness, a misunderstanding, a miscommunication, or a minor accident. Hopefully, we soon make it back into the cool forest together, wiser about the ways of the world and the vast web of life. We can laugh about it together now, because we love each other.

Sometimes we just need forgiveness, unmerited grace. One time, near Tofte on a perfectly marvelous day, I was walking on a downhill section of the trail coming off of a ridge. It happened so quickly, I am not sure of the cause. Maybe some loose rocks or a root, but most likely it was carelessness, just striding too fast for the terrain, not paying close attention to what was right before me. And I fell.

It happened so quickly. I couldn't seem to stop myself. I fell hard, tumbled down the hill and off the trail and into a little ravine. I ended up on my back on top of my backpack, head down the hill, and for a moment I could not get up. I couldn't get the right leverage. I knew that Shirley would soon be coming along and even though I could have used some help, I didn't want her to see me like this. Was I getting too old to hike; was my coordination gone? I was angry and embarrassed. I really needed a hug, but I didn't want help. It was a crisis of pride and fear, lying there not knowing how much damage I had done to myself. But with child raising, in those moments of poor judgment and stupid mistakes, when we stumble and it's our own selfish fault, the question is not just what damage have I done to myself in the fall but what damage have I done to others. God, we need forgiveness in this journey together. And the good shepherd offers amazing grace!

Often, we need each other for a different, more complete perspective. One day, on the trail near Alfred's Pond, while hiking through a thick willow marsh over a flooded trail, I startled a moose. In that thicket of vegetation, maybe ten feet from me, the moose also scared the heck out of me as it crashed through the willows, reeds, and water. In that wet thicket of green I couldn't see what was happening. I didn't really know what was going on. I was startled, confused. But Shirley, from a different perspective, just twenty feet away, caught a glimpse of this whole drama. She could make sense out of all this for me. When she stopped laughing, she could complete the story for me — my story. In child raising we need each other — a spouse hopefully, or grandparent, sponsor, friends, teachers, a congregation. We need others for a more complete perspective of this crucial, life-forming and life-giving drama that we are in together, in welcoming children into the peace of God.

Being a "good" mother and a "good" father, is not an easy task. But there is also grand epiphany. Repeatedly on the Superior Hiking Trail, a hot, routine section of the dense forest trail would all of a sudden (and it was always a moment of wonder), open up to the grand vista of Lake Superior — a vast array of blue. An endless blue is up north of here with no sight of Wisconsin. It would be just the hazy blue of water and sky meeting in perfect harmony. Or it would be the surprise of a thundering cascade of agitated water cutting its way through the red rhyolite rocks — cool and alive, and rushing toward its home in the sea. You just know this journey has some divine implications.

It's in this journey, and not the destination, that one is truly enveloped in beauty and divine purpose. Raising the child as a loving parent, a close friend, a Sunday school teacher, a citizen working for schools that integrate learning and values-based living — it is a sacrifice for the well-being of the other, but it also gives you life back in return, in being part of the promise that divine love will never abandon.

Jesus could have said, "I am the good mother, the good father, the good parent, who gives her life for the child."

Jesus, as Emmanuel — God-with-us — also broadened the definition of who our child is! We have the responsibility and privilege now to see all children as our children — the whole flock as our own to protect, cherish, nourish, respect, and embrace in love. If we wish to model Jesus, then all others become our child, our parent, our mother, father, sister, and brother — our family in whom we can see the very image of God. When we enter this desire for co-humanity within the reality of the eternity of God's love, then the long hike becomes a blessed journey in any kind of weather. It is a blessing knowing that mother and son and father and daughter can never be ultimately separated by selfishness or destiny.

"I am the good mother. I want only the best that only love can offer you, my sacred child."

We thank you — our mothers — for those frequent moments when you reflect the very nature of God.

> *"I am the good shepherd," said Jesus. "The good shepherd lays down his life for all the sheep; for all the sacred children."* — John 10:11 (paraphrased)

Amen.

Sermon delivered May 14, 2000
First Lutheran Church
Duluth, Minnesota

_____

1. Sue Miller, *The Good Mother* (New York: Dell Publishing, 1986).

Last Lecture

> *I still have many things to say to you, but you cannot bear them now. When the Spirit of truth comes, he will guide you into all the truth; for he will not speak on his own, but will speak whatever he hears, and he will declare to you the things that are to come. He will glorify me, because he will take what is mine and declare it to you. All that the Father has is mine. For this reason I said that he will take what is mine and declare it to you.* — John 16:12-15

This text (according to the book of Saint John) is a section of Jesus' final speech to his followers in Jerusalem just before his arrest and trial and execution. Jesus gathered his followers on the very threshold of his death and attempted to tell them what his ministry — what his life — had been all about. He tried to tell them precisely the most important things. But he also knew them well, and said to them in that final sermon, "I still have so many things to say to you, but I know you cannot comprehend or emotionally understand them all at this moment. But the Spirit of truth will come, and this presence of God will be there for you, to guide you into the future. All that God, the Creator, the loving parent, has in mind, and it is offered to you."

It used to be quite common in colleges for campus ministry programs or the student philosophy club to sponsor a "last lecture series." The students and I, for example, would pick out a few of the most popular and respected faculty members and invite them to participate in the series. We would ask each of them to give a lecture on a separate evening with a decision following. These were the instructions to the speakers: We want you to pretend that you

93

are soon going to die. You only have enough strength, energy, and time left to give one final lecture. Your students and colleagues will gather for this, your "last lecture." What do you want to say to us? We want to know! What will your final words be to us in your last speech?

If the professor was an astrophysicist, for example, and decided in the last lecture to tell us with the best clarity possible about "gravitational lensing" or "globular star clusters" or "the limitations of the Hubble Space Telescope," for example, no matter how articulate and engaging such a lecture would be, if that's all they said, we would be very disappointed. We wanted them, on their deathbed, to tell us what they believe to be the meaning of life. What gave them hope (if they had any), what truth about life and death and God could they pass on to us? "Come on, this is your last lecture, the last opportunity to tell us what your mind, and life experience, and soul know about truth, about what we are all about as human beings!"

Today's gospel text is a part of Jesus' last lecture before his death. The disciples thought they saw God present in Jesus, but the tension and danger is building in Jerusalem. We fear for your safety, Jesus. Don't leave us. Don't abandon us, Jesus! Don't abandon us, dear God.

For many of the college students, I am afraid, that last lecture series was viewed as a game, as interesting entertainment. For most faculty who understood the nature of the invitation, took it seriously, and then actually accepted the invitation to speak, that last lecture was something to wrestle with, to struggle with to get it right, to say what they really held to be of utmost importance — what they held to be dear and needed to share.

And although this concept of a "last lecture" is not something that pertains to one age group more than another age group, it does seem that the older we get, if we are honest and thoughtful, the more closely we listen to the offered insights given in "last lectures." What is it in life that gives lasting meaning that people of vast experience can share? What is it that they have lived for, that they believe has permanent meaning; that they want to pass on to their children or to others over whom they have some influence?

Maybe the urgency increases as we get older because of those instructions for the last lecture, where it says, "You will soon die," so tell us what it is that you hold most dear. As we face death, knowing the meaning of life becomes more urgent.

I think what got me in this mood is that I recently had my "annual" physical exam. What with the impending move to Duluth, and then the time-consuming necessity to become acclimated to my new job, I hadn't had a thorough physical exam for a couple of years, and I ran out of excuses. I made an appointment and went to be poked, probed, and bled. Even though my physician here is very kind, he could not totally mask the truth in his comments that at least parts of me are becoming rather old. "The casings for tendons and muscles in your shoulder are a bit worn, a bit frayed, from long years of use. And there is some nerve damage that is chronic. Your skin has become thin from all those summers in the sun."

Well, I think it's true about me being thin-skinned. Perhaps I am sensitive about this because the president of the United States is my age, and he has recently been calling himself "near elderly." (Which I guess is better than being called "no spring chicken" or a "pre-geezer.") And there have been a number of articles lately about us baby boomers having occasional "senior moments" — memory problems, hearing loss, bifocals. Calling us "junior seniors" or the "mature market" doesn't help much either.

Maybe all this is just a midlife crisis, even though, as my son put it the other day, "Dad, I think you are older than midlife."

Actually, it was about twelve years ago now, that I was working late one winter night on some writing assignment, when I realized that our manufactured *chronos* time had moved beyond midnight and into the day of my birthday. Our human desire to encapsulate and measure time movement indicated that something had changed. The earth had revolved into another day, no longer the fifteenth of February but now the sixteenth, and I was then forty years old — over forty years since my first breath. And then it popped into my early morning fatigued mind, "Forty years old. Forty years old! That's half way to death!" Actually, according to actuary charts, American males on average live to their mid-seventies or so, and I was then forty and definitely *more* than halfway to death.

I desperately wanted some image to pull me out of a mounting anxiety. I was drinking Classic Coke for the caffeine to stay awake to finish my evening work. I held in my hand a half-filled bottle of Coke. Half finished. I was like a half finished bottle of soda. And often, the second half loses its fizz. I watched its bubbles escape into the void of the dark room. Its effervescence and kinetic energy was going fast. Stale already. Flat, as in "flat brain waves." Often one cannot finish the end of the bottle. It is dumped out. Down the drain.

What pulled me out of that late night bout with mortality and mounting despair was a quick decision to live until 100. But now I am 52, and I can't out run this by doubling my age anymore. I was privileged to perform the funeral of a fine woman last week, one of our fellow members, Nellie Shay. Nellie was 100 years old at the time of her death. She had enjoyed her 100th birthday party in relatively good health, surrounded by family and friends, and then just a few days later had a stroke, and died calmly in her sleep. When Nellie's obituary appeared in the paper, it stated that she was 100 years old; but right next to her obituary was the obituary of another woman who died at 106. I started thinking that poor Nellie had died in her prime, before her time! Maybe I should plan to live to 106 and then I would no longer be halfway to death.

This reminded me of a confirmation exercise where ninth grade students are asked as a homework assignment to write their own obituaries. The hope is that this will get them to think about what is most important in life, and think about ways that they could serve God in their future occupations and family building. One student wrote this obituary: "James McLaughlin, age 99, former power broker, died instantly and painlessly Monday after a vigorous game of tennis at this summer mansion in Malibu, California. He was a graduate of Harvard University, which he owned." I think he missed the whole point of the exercise, just like I had.

But Nellie Shay offered me a reminder last week to look beyond each such fear and foolishness. Nellie apparently lived her life, as story after story about her revealed, as a collage of faithful and loving acts. That was the story told of her life, and it didn't ultimately matter if she had lived to be twenty or 100 years of age.

Her story happened to be a century of faith. Her assurance in the presence of God, and in her call to be Christlike to all she encountered was summarized as "a century of faith," but the number of years had nothing to do with what we celebrated at her funeral. Death is still the enemy at twenty or 100; but what we celebrated at her funeral was the stability of her life as faith-grounded, along with the kept promises of God — promises kept for all of us at any age, forever.

We are all, of course, at any age, dying; we are all on the threshold of death; our lives are always a precious, momentary gift. In that last lecture of Jesus in the book of Saint John, the story was told again about the love of God as lived by Jesus, and the everlasting gift of the Holy Spirit — the Spirit of truth — that will never abandon us as we face death, or the new job, or the responsibility of child raising, or any storm. Any storm, at any age. This I how I envision that last lecture of Jesus.

Many art museums today have set aside exhibit space, often a room or more, for what is called "video art." This artwork includes one or more screens or monitors where video images can be viewed in a controlled setting. One of the best known of these video artists is Bill Viola who, at the moment, has a major show in progress at the Whitney Museum in New York. One of Viola's works is titled, "Room for Saint John of the Cross." This historical Saint John was a holy man who was imprisoned during the Inquisition. He was tortured and threatened with death day after day. But even on the edge of death, he wrote poems that were in a sense, his "last lecture." In Viola's video artwork, the viewer walks into a large, dark room with a screen occupying an entire wall on which is being projected a film of mountains in a raging, violent storm — thunder and lightning and wind were too strong for it to stay steady. Even the mountains themselves seem to be in turmoil — unstable, shaking. In the middle of this room is a small jail cell with a bare, raw glowing incandescent light. Inside the cell is a jug on a table and sawdust on the floor, and when you come close you can hear a recording of a man whispering those poems of Saint John, poems about Jesus, and the God of creation, and the real presence of God in his life. Also on the table in the cell is a small video monitor that is showing a film of the same mountains as on the wall outside the cell, but this picture is steady, the mountains are firmly rooted, and they are drenched in summer sunlight. *There is no storm.* You don't need to know anything about Saint John of the Cross to get the message that here was a man that through a living faith was also grounded, even on the edge of death, at peace. And it all has nothing to do with age.

The meaning of today's gospel text — these words from Jesus' last lecture — that is, even in death and physical departing, God's presence is not diminished but is enhanced. The Creator God of all existence, revealed to us in the life of Jesus, cares about us personally, and is there for us now, willing to guide us and love us forever. This is the Trinitarian understanding of God — Father, Son, and Holy Spirit — the firm foundation of the God of the totality of reality offering to form your last lecture, which can be lived now, modeling Jesus — forgiven, guided, held securely by the living, engaging Spirit of truth — the reality of God alive that can still any storm at any age or stage of life.

From the last lecture of Jesus, spoken in the shadow of Golgatha:

> *I still have so many things to say to you, but I know you cannot fully understand them all at this moment. But the Spirit of truth comes, and this Spirit of God is there for you, to guide you into all truth. All that God, the Creator-Father, has is mine, and it is offered to you.*
> — John 16:12-15 (paraphrased)

Thanks be to God! Holy, holy, holy! Not halfway to death, but all the way to life. Father, Son and engaging Spirit of Truth. Amen.

Sermon delivered June 7, 1998
First Lutheran Church
Duluth, Minnesota

About The Author

Born and raised at the Jersey Shore, Michael David Wuchter earned his undergraduate degree at Wittenberg University in Springfield, Ohio, then returned to the East for his Master of Divinity degree from the Lutheran Theological Seminary in Philadelphia, Pennsylvania, and his Doctorate of Ministry Degree from Princeton Theological Seminary. He became a third-generation Lutheran pastor. Wittenberg University honored him for meritorious service in 1983 and he was a Fulbright Scholar in India in the summer of 1984.

Michael Wuchter served Resurrection Lutheran Church in Hamilton Square, New Jersey, from 1972-1979. Wittenberg University, where both he and his wife, Shirley, had been students, called him to become the Pastor to the University in 1979. He served eighteen years as campus pastor before moving back to a parish setting in Duluth, Minnesota. Three years later, while on a mission trip to a companion congregation in Oniipi, Namibia, Africa, his life ended unexpectedly at age 54 on August 5, 2000.

Shirley resides in Duluth. The Wuchters' son, Andrew, and his wife, Traci, also live in Minnesota. The Wuchters' daughter, Kirsten, her husband, Bob, their daughter, Eleanor Grace, and their new baby, Hannah Ruth, live in Montana.